THE SECRET SACRED

THE SECRET SACRED

MYSTERY CULTS IN ANCIENT GREECE AND ROME

DAMIEN STONE

REAKTION BOOKS

Published by
REAKTION BOOKS LTD
2–4 Sebastian Street
London EC1V 0HE, UK
www.reaktionbooks.co.uk

First published 2025

EU GPSR Authorised Representative
Logos Europe, 9 rue Nicolas Poussin, 17000, La Rochelle, France
email: contact@logoseurope.eu

Printed and bound in Great Britain by Bell & Bain, Glasgow

A catalogue record for this book is available from the British Library

ISBN 978 1 83639 109 8

CONTENTS

Detail from Apulian red-figure bell krater depicting a maenad and satyr parading at night, *c.* 380–365 BC. She holds two flaming torches, while he wields a pail and thyrsus.

ONE

WHAT IS A MYSTERY RELIGION?

'Mystery religions' refers to the various cults of Classical antiquity that offered secret wisdom to their members. Known by the Greek term *mysteria* and the Latin *mysterium*, the name given to these religious experiences appears to derive from the Hittite verb *munnae*, meaning 'to conceal', 'to hide' or 'to shut out of sight'.[1] For these were special rites concealed from public view and gave access to hidden knowledge. Knowledge of the beliefs and practices of the Mysteries required initiation, also referred to as *orgia* or *teletai*.[2] Initiation was a rite of passage that fundamentally changed the status of a person who emerged as a *mystes*. Our word 'initiate' derives from the Latin term used by the Romans to describe individuals who had undergone such an experience. An *initiatus* was 'one who has gone in'.[3] The Mysteries offered an alternative and ecstatic religious experience to the official cults of Greek and Roman civic religion. It was not an either/or situation, but rather a supplement. An individual could participate in the state religion and be initiated into one or multiple of these elective cults. These tended to be exclusive communities, requiring payment of an initiation fee and sometimes ongoing offerings to the associated gods of a cult. In exchange, an initiate received a more intimate and direct religious experience with the divine.

Standard Classical religion was polytheistic, revolving around an assembly of anthropomorphic immortal deities led by a kingly sky god called Zeus by the Greeks and Jupiter by the Romans. Fellow gods included his wife Hera (Juno), his son the messenger Hermes (Mercury) and his brother Hades (Pluto), lord of the Underworld. These gods often had animals or other symbols associated with them. For wise Athena (Minerva), these were the owl and the olive tree, with a warrior's helmet and a snake-covered breastplate known as the *aegis* being her dress of choice. Such attributes help identify them in artistic depictions. Divine beings also came to personify concepts like Victory, Justice and Memory. Some were quite specific, Vagitanus being the Roman god who opened a newborn's mouth for their first cry.[4] The gods presided over all components that were understood to make up the universe: in the wildness of nature, in the public functioning of the city and in the privacy of the household. They also assisted passage to and ruled over the world beyond, a divine function of key importance in mystery cults. The gods decided an individual's fate, determining success or failure in commerce enterprises, on the battlefield and in the production of healthy children. They could cause illness and death, or provide a cure for affliction. Rituals designed to maintain sound relations with the divine were thus embedded in daily practice and a wider calendar of festivals. Complex mythological narratives were told about this large, squabbling family of anthropomorphic heavenly beings. Mystery religions developed these established tales, sometimes reworking

As well as being a god of commerce, travellers and thieves, Hermes also assisted those making their final journey to the land of the dead. This role as the Psychopomos ('Guide of Souls') is illustrated by Adolf Hirémy-Hirschl in the 1898 painting *Souls on the Banks of the Acheron*.

them into alternative mythologies that elevated the positions of certain gods. These sacred narratives provided context for rituals and would likely have taken on additional meaning for initiates, who performed actions that replicated events from the lives of the gods. Mystery cults that adopted a foreign deity as their patron rather uniquely blended a mix of Classical motifs and those perceived as 'Eastern' in their style and stories.

Conventional Classical temples housed a cult statue of a deity that was concealed in darkness within the building and attended upon by priests. Though such statues were rendered by human hands, the gods were believed to inhabit them. Great power was thus assigned to these sculptures, made of chryselephantine (ivory and gold), bronze or marble. Particularly old and revered were *xoana*, wooden effigies or aniconic images of deities. Rites were conducted at the altar, outside the temple and directly in front of the building. The gods were distant figures whose relationship with humanity was largely transactional. Devotees could offer sacrifices and other votive offerings at the altar in regular public acts of display. By contrast, sacred spaces in which the mysteries were conducted were often congregational, and within them individuals were inducted and participated in the secret rites. Here mythological stories were re-enacted, holy objects and images revealed, and sacred substances consumed. In contrast to a routinely repeated ritual (as occurs in the case of a weekly church service), they were highly charged events that were conducted occasionally.[5] Though infrequent, they were memorable for their intensity. Space and time demarcated the secret and sacred. The mystic rites were frequently conducted at night with sound and light used dramatically to create a sensory experience that was both awesome and terrifying. Dio Chrysostom (first century AD) reports the experience of an initiate who was taken to 'some mystic chamber extraordinary in beauty and size, where he would see many mystic sights and hear many such sounds, with darkness and light appearing to him in alternation, and thousands of other things taking place'.[6] Though indicative of an awe-inspiring spectacle, it provides no specific information on the associated beliefs, meaning and motivation for being initiated. On leaving, an initiate was expected not to discuss what he/she had witnessed and what esoteric knowledge had been attained.

Most Classical authors therefore remained silent on the subject. Any information given is too often cut short, as in a passage of the ancient Greek travel writer Pausanias (second century AD) that tantalizes us with the statement, 'I must say nothing, for its story is a holy mystery.'[7] Pausanias' very useful work describes multiple sanctuaries with clandestine practices, and he may have been inducted into various cults during his sojourn around the Hellenic world. Some aspects of mystery religions were widely known and could be discussed, while other parts of the ceremonies were reserved only for initiates. There are cases recorded of punishments being exacted on individuals who divulged secrets of the Mysteries to the uninitiated.[8] Fuller descriptions of the sacred rites survive in the accounts of Christian apologists that attempted to out, ridicule and condemn the practices. Though helpful, showing knowledge of myths and passwords used in cultic ritual, these are very biased sources.

Archaeology offers further clues in surviving images of stories and rituals related to the Mysteries, as well as the sites where they were conducted. By being initiated, the Mystery cults taught followers how to understand these images, which may not have been fully comprehended by non-members who saw them. For example, the sacred statue of the unique form of Artemis (Diana) venerated at Ephesus is depicted on coins minted from that city. This does not mean that those who carried them in their pocket (Ephesus being an important trading port) necessarily understood the exact nature of the many globules that cover the goddess' chest. They have been variously interpreted by modern scholars as breasts, sacrificial bulls' testicles, eggs, a cluster of grapes

Marble sculpture of Ephesian Artemis, 2nd century AD.

or bags from which she distributed gifts. Only those initiated into her cult are likely to have truly understood the exact significance of this iconographic peculiarity of Ephesian Artemis.[9] That said, much of that witnessed by the initiates of the various mystery cults was probably beyond their understanding or could not be put into words. Such a mystery element is most apparent in a festival of Athena known as the *Arrhephoria*, in which girls were given something to carry upon their heads. Neither they, nor the priestess of Athena who gave it to them, knew what this mystery object was.[10]

While induction frequently occurred in the context of festivals conducted by cult officials, there were also private initiators who could be employed by individuals. As opposed to mysteries that were tied to specific places, these itinerant workers could bring secret revelations from the gods to you. Glaucothea, the mother of the famed Athenian orator Demosthenes (fourth century BC), was known for offering such a service. He is reported to have assisted her in doing so: scrubbing the initiates' bodies in clay that had been mixed with wheat grain, assisting them to dress in fawn skins and reading sacred words from a scroll that climaxed in the statement, 'I have escaped the bad; I have found the better.'[11] Glaucothea's initiated then paraded through the streets waving writhing snakes in their hands and wearing wreaths upon their heads. In this example our sources do not report the name of the associated god, but Dionysus is a likely candidate.

Though the specifics may elude us today, these cults enhanced people's lives with meaning not available in standard civic religion. Several of the mystery religions seem to have offered benefits that transcended this world, rewarding the initiated in the afterlife. Hugh Bowden, a prominent scholar of ancient Greek religion, has proposed that such descriptions of a happy hereafter parallel those promised to Menelaus in Homer (*Odyssey* IV.565–8) for marrying into the family of the gods. This contrasts with the gloomy nature of the Underworld allotted to the masses as described later in Book XI of the *Odyssey*, a joyless place situated in murky darkness. 'The afterlife promised to initiates looks very similar to that of Menelaus, and the explanation of it is the same: like Menelaus, initiates have been in close contact with a god.'[12] By taking Helen as his wife, he becomes Zeus' son-in-law, and is thus granted special access to an exclusive area in the afterlife for heroes known as the Elysian Fields. Bowden argues that the major appeal of mystery cults was a more personal relationship with the divine and that salvation after death probably wasn't a major enticement for initiates, but rather an added bonus. As we will see, though, for at least some cults there is evidence that the promise of a better afterlife was desirable. In the case of Orphic-Bacchic Mysteries, this influenced the material culture with which initiates were buried after death.

*

THIS BOOK AIMS to provide an introduction to the Mysteries for a general reader. In each of the following chapters, a combination of written and visual sources is used to interpret each of the major mystery cults of Greece and Rome. The initial chapters each examine the three best-known mysteries from antiquity: those of Demeter at Eleusis, those of Isis and those of Mithras. Chapter Five examines a mystery religion based at Samothrace that had much fame in antiquity, but is less familiar to audiences today. In Chapters Six and Seven we move from mystery practices within temple sanctuaries to those of itinerant worship conducted outdoors. In Chapter Eight we will examine two Roman instances illustrating cults that were critiqued by contemporaries and short-lived. Our final chapter looks at the potential influence on early Christianity and remnants of mystery religions that permeate our world today. In addition to the major mystery religions examined, there are many fleeting references to small localized cults on which information is too limited for discussion in this book. There are likely to have been more, of which no traces survive. As a matter of convention, the Greek name is given preference when referring to deities in this book, with the later Roman names included in brackets as a divine figure is first introduced. A glossary of gods that feature in the Mysteries is included at the back of this book for the convenience of the reader.

Hades abducts Persephone in his chariot at the centre of this Apulian red-figure hydria, 340–330 BC. Divine figures surround, including Demeter on the lower left. She runs in search of her daughter with her arms raised in a gesture of grief, wielding a cross-torch in one hand.

TWO

DEMETER, PERSEPHONE AND THE ELEUSINIAN MYSTERIES

The most famous of all mystery religions was that centred on the site of Eleusis, located in Attica about 20 kilometres (12 mi.) northwest of Athens. Sacred rites there were associated with the agrarian goddess Demeter (Ceres) and her daughter Persephone (Proserpina), conducted inside a temple known as the Telesterion. Classical authors often referred to Persephone by the alternative name of Kore ('The Maiden'). Marcus Tullius Cicero (first century BC) declared that Athens had given 'nothing finer' to humanity than the Mysteries, for 'we learn in them the basic principles of life, and from them acquire not only a way of living in happiness but also a way of dying with greater hope.'[1] Crinagoras of Mytilene (first century BC) wrote that even if a person was to travel nowhere else, they should go to Eleusis to experience the festival of Demeter, for 'then your heart may be free of care while you live, and lighter when you go to the land of the dead.'[2] This must-see destination drew in pilgrims from around the Greek and later Roman world. Its prestige saw other Classical cities named after Eleusis. A suburb of Alexandria in Egypt likewise bore its name, with a branch replicating the Eleusinian Mysteries being set up by Ptolemy I to increase the status of his Hellenistic city.[3]

The Eleusinian Mysteries were performed for over 1,000 years. Their foundations may be in an agrarian cult of the Bronze Age, with excavations beneath the sanctuary revealing Mycenaean remains.[4] These, however, were abandoned with the demise of that civilization at the end of the thirteenth century BC. The settlement was not reoccupied until the eighth century BC. The Mysteries were then continuously practised, until Christianity came to dominate the Roman religious scene and they declined. It ended for Eleusis when the site was sacked by the Visigoths at the end of fourth century AD.[5]

The requirements for initiation were being able to speak Greek (thus not a 'barbarian') and being free of blood-guilt (pollution that adhered to individuals who had committed murder).[6] Members also had to swear a vow of secrecy. Romans became permitted to partake in the Mysteries once Athens had been added to their empire (much to the joy of many a Roman emperor, including the Greece-loving Hadrian). Both men and women (including slaves) could be initiated and participate in the ceremonies. These rituals appear to have involved the retelling and emulation of elements from the mythological story of Demeter and Persephone. The best version of this is preserved in the Homeric Hymn to Demeter, written about 650–550 BC.[7]

THE HOMERIC HYMN TO DEMETER

This tale begins with the abduction of Persephone by the god of the Underworld, Hades (Pluto). While she is picking flowers in a field with a group of other maidens, Hades rises out of the earth on a golden chariot and drags her down to the land of the dead. There, with the permission of his brother Zeus (Jupiter), she is made Hades' wife and queen of the Underworld. Demeter, hearing Persephone's screams and unable to find her daughter, is distraught. She does not consume the sacred foods of the gods, ambrosia and nectar. She does not bathe. Bearing flaming torches to guide her path, she searches the Earth. She is eventually told by Helios (Sol), the all-seeing Sun, of her daughter's fate. Angry at the Olympian gods for allowing this to happen, she abandons her divine posting and takes on mortal form. Disguised as an old woman, she eventually arrives at Eleusis. Sitting beside the Maiden's Well she is approached by the four daughters of the local ruler Celeus and his wife Metaneira. They take her back to the palace, where she becomes nurse to the king and queen's infant son, Demophoön.

On arrival, Demeter (referring to herself by the pseudonym Doso) is offered wine by Metaneira. She refuses, instead ordering the queen to prepare for her the *kykeon*, a beverage described as being made of mixed barley, water and mint. Demeter accepts and drinks the concoction before Demophoön is put under her protection. The goddess begins a routine of some rather unorthodox childcare:

> Demeter anointed him with ambrosia as though he were born from a god, breathing on him sweetly as she held him to her breast. At night she buried him in the heart of the fire, like a torch, without his parents knowing. It was a great wonder to them how he

> grew far beyond his years, and he was in appearance like a god.[8]

However, Demeter's intentions to make him ageless and deathless are unfortunately thwarted by the curious Metaneira. At night the queen spies upon the nurse in her employ, and screams with terror at seeing her baby apparently being roasted upon a fire. Demeter is enraged at Metaneira's interruption and ignorance. She withdraws Demophoön from the flames that were burning away his mortality and throws him on the ground. Though he is denied godhood, Metaneira is told that Demophoön will flourish as a mortal and be honoured because he has slept in the arms of a goddess.

Dropping the guise of Doso, Demeter reveals her divinity. Throwing away the visage of old age, she becomes beautiful and terrifying. She grows in stature and her hair shines golden. Pleasant fragrance drifts from her body and she emits light that flashes like lightning through the palace. Before leaving, the goddess instructs the Eleusinians to build a temple for her in their city. Here, she says, 'I myself will inaugurate my mysteries, so that from now on you may perform them in all purity and be reconciled to my heart.'[9] Celeus, keen to regain favour with the goddess, follows her command and the sanctuary to Demeter is founded. Into her temple she withdraws.

Demeter continues to grieve for her daughter and, as goddess of grain, is able to render the Earth barren. Failing crops result in starvation for humankind. Without food, altars of the gods are also denied their usual sacrifices. Zeus finally decides to intervene. He sends Iris, messenger goddess and personification of the rainbow, to retrieve Demeter from Eleusis. Unable to convince her, each of the Olympian gods then approach Demeter one by one, attempting to placate her with praise and various gifts. But she stubbornly refuses to go back to Olympus until her daughter has been returned from the Underworld. Zeus therefore sends another messenger god, the wing-sandalled Hermes (Mercury), down to Hades with orders that Persephone must be given back. Hermes here performs his role as Psychopompos, the guider of souls who assists the dead by safely escorting them between this world and the next. This key function of the

Persephone ascends from the Underworld escorted by Hermes. Hekate, wielding two flaming torches, leads the maiden towards her mother, Demeter, on the right. Attic red-figure bell krater, *c.* 440 BC.

god was evoked by multiple mystery religions that provided their initiates with an enhanced understanding of the Underworld. Hekate, as a goddess of boundaries and magic, also assists in the search and retrieval of Persephone. As it is the command of Zeus, Hades must comply and feigns a willingness to return Demeter's daughter. He tells Persephone that he is not an unworthy husband. As Queen of the Underworld, says Hades, 'There will be eternal punishment for those who do wrong and do not ritually appease your spirit by performing sacred rites and making due offerings.'[10] Before she departs with Hermes, Hades secretly gives her seeds of the pomegranate, from which she eats.

Persephone is taken to be reunited with Demeter at her temple at Eleusis. The grain goddess is ecstatic at the return and embraces her daughter. Suspicion suddenly grips Demeter, however, as she knows Hades is unlikely to acquiesce so easily. Persephone is asked if she consumed any food while in the Underworld and responds that she was forced to eat from the pomegranate against her will. Because she ate food in the Underworld, Persephone will be required to live one-third of each year in the Underworld, returning to the upper world with the arrival of springtime. Though Demeter restores the earth's fertility, it is rendered barren again each winter when the she goes into mourning at the annual descent of her daughter to Hades (this being an aetiological myth that explained the change of the seasons).

Demeter then sets about establishing the Eleusinian Mysteries in her purpose-built temple. She inducts a group of leaders, instructing them in how to correctly perform her secret and holy rites. For these were

Triptolemus and Persephone, tondo of a red-figure Attic cup found at Vulci, *c.* 470–460 BC.

> sacred mysteries which no one may transgress in any way or inquire into or speak about, for great awe of the gods stops the voice. Blessed is the one of all the people on the earth who has seen these mysteries. But whoever is not initiated into the rites, whoever has no part in them, that person never shares the same fate when he dies and goes down to the gloom and darkness below.[11]

Demeter and Persephone then ascend to their place at Olympus. As the hymn draws to conclusion, a key figure associated with the traditions and art of the Eleusinian Mysteries is also introduced, though only in passing. Among the names of the original priests of Demeter, a certain Triptolemus is named as one of the first men to learn her secret rites. He is often confused with his younger brother Demophoön, perhaps due to the latter's memorable role as being the divinely barbecued baby of the myth. Triptolemus becomes the messenger of Demeter. Riding upon a serpent-drawn chariot, he shares and spreads her agricultural arts. The cycle of descent, search and ascent within the myth were to be central in the Mysteries, with an emphasis on the final stage – the climatic ascent of the initiated.

THE FESTIVAL

Isocrates (fifth–fourth century BC) writes that

> When Demeter was wandering about after Kore had been taken from her, she came to our land. She was well disposed towards our ancestors because of the kindnesses they showed her, which none but initiates may hear, and she gave them the two greatest gifts of all: crops, which have distinguished our life from that of animals, and the Mysteries, which have given their participants sweeter hopes for the end of life and indeed for all our existence.[12]

The vast span of time over which the Mysteries were practised saw some modifications in different periods, but our rough understanding of how this divine gift was enacted is as follows.

Proceedings were administrated by two families of Eleusis: the Eumolpidae (descendants of the legendary King Eumolpus, whose name means 'untainted by blame') and the Kerykes ('heralds').[13] Prior to the festival, these families sent out messengers to all major Greek cities, declaring a sacred truce and safe passage to anyone wanting to travel to Attica for the occasion. There seems to have been a separate Eleusinian festival conducted some time prior to the major ceremonies, which was known as the Lesser Mysteries. Diodorus Siculus (first century BC) claims that the Lesser Mysteries were first introduced by Demeter so that Herakles could be purified after slaying the centaurs.[14] These lesser rites are not well understood, but appear to have been a one-day preparatory prerequisite.[15] The Hellenistic ruler Demetrius I of Macedon (337–283 BC) apparently had his subject Athenians twice rename the months to enable him to participate in the Lesser and then the Greater Mysteries within a few days of each other.[16] That it was exceptional for one to skip this step is apparent in a remark from Socrates that was recorded by Plato (fifth–fourth century BC): 'You are fortunate in that you have been initiated into the Great before the Little: I did not think that that was permitted.'[17]

The greater festival, in which the secret mystery rites were embedded, was conducted over nine days in the Greek month of Boedromion (roughly around the end of September and the beginning of October).[18] This was an annual occurrence, with every fourth year being a particularly splendid celebration. Conducting the various rituals that made up the multi-day programme were a group of both male and female religious officials. The two most important were the High Priestess of Demeter and a High Priest known as the Hierophant. These were inherited positions drawn from the eminent Eleusinian families. During the rites, the High

Priestess appears to have embodied the role of both the goddesses Demeter and Persephone.[19] The name of the current High Priestess was used in inscriptions for the dating of events at Eleusis.[20]

The festival commenced in Athens, and was conducted in public view. The necessity of secrecy would be adopted later during the main rites conducted within the sanctuary at Eleusis itself. These were only experienced by returning initiates and those being initiated for the first time. The day before the festival began, a procession of priests and priestesses left Eleusis carrying the *hiera*, holy objects that were concealed in containers (known as *cista*) that were tied with red ribbons.[21] A military escort accompanied them to a 'branch' sanctuary on the slopes of the Athenian Acropolis known as the City Eleusinion.[22] The form of these sacred artefacts is unfortunately unknown, but Pausanias describes the building where they were housed during their sojourn in Athens. The City Eleusinion contained cult images of Demeter and Persephone, alongside a statue of the daimon Iakkhos holding a torch.[23] Iakkhos was the god of the ritual cry of joy (*iakhe*) shouted by participants of Eleusinian Mysteries during procession. The chorus of ecstatic initiates encountered in the Underworld by Dionysus in Aristophanes' play *The Frogs* thus heap praise on the divine torch-bearer in song:

> Oh Iakkhos! Power excelling, here in stately temples dwelling. Oh Iakkhos! Oh lakkhos! Come to tread this verdant level, come to dance in mystic revel, come whilst round thy forehead hurtles many a wreath of fruitful myrtles, come with wild and saucy paces

> mingling in our joyous dance, pure and holy, which embraces all the charms of all the Graces . . . Come, arise, from sleep awaking, come the fiery torches shaking . . . Call him hither without delay, him who travels with his Chorus, dancing along on the Sacred Way. Oh come with the joy of thy festival song, Oh come to the goddess, Oh mix with our throng . . . Oh Lord of the frolic and dance, Iakkhos, beside me advance![24]

Iakkhos was seen as the Eleusinian aspect of the rapturous god of wine Dionysus. Nearby the City Eleusinion was another temple to Triptolemus, Demeter's agriculture-spreading disciple. Pausanias does cut us short on details, however: 'After I had intended to go further into the story [of Triptolemus and Demeter], and to describe the contents of the sanctuary at Athens called the Eleusinion, I was stayed by a vision in a dream. I shall therefore turn to those things it is lawful to write of to all men.'[25]

The festival proper began with a proclamation read out in Athens, summoning participants to come celebrate the Mysteries in Eleusis. On the second day, participants took piglets to the sea and washed them in the waters of the Aegean. Returning to the city with a wriggling, oinking animal, each individual sacrificed their piglet as a form of purification.[26] The piglet was an animal particularly associated with the worship of Demeter and Persephone. Pigs were regarded as symbols of fertility, due to their capability to produce large litters of offspring. This also made them an affordable choice of animal for sacrifice. When death is decreed for a character in Aristophanes' play *Peace*, he requests, 'lend me three drachmae to buy a young pig; I wish to have myself initiated before I die.'[27] The reference is to Eleusis, initiation being desired prior to death for its after-life benefits. Though not mentioned in the Homeric Hymn, other mythological accounts relate that a swineherd named Eubouleus witnessed the abduction of Persephone. The poor farmer's pigs were swallowed up by the earth when Hades opened the Underworld to seize her.[28] Not only live offerings, but small votive ceramic piglet figures and large marble sculptures of swine were presented to the goddesses at Eleusis. The sacrifice of pigs into pits played a key role in another festival to Demeter and her daughter called the Thesmophoria.[29] Interestingly, the ancient Greek word commonly used for a young pig was *choiros*. This term was also used in reference to the vulva of a young woman.[30] Piglet sacrifices and pig-shaped votive offerings were therefore also appropriate offerings that were made by nubile girls to Demeter and Persephone prior to their wedding.

Further sacrifices were conducted to various gods in Athens during the third and fourth days.[31] It was now that the festival moved to Eleusis. On the fifth and sixth days, a procession advanced along the Sacred Way, the road leading to Eleusis. The *hiera* were carried back by the Eleusinian priests and priestesses. Then came the initiates themselves. Festively dressed, each was crowned with a wreath of myrtle.[32] They were led by a statue of Iakkhos and jubilantly called out his name: Iakhe, Iakhe! During the long walk there were several checkpoints where participants paused for ritual activities. At the Rheitoi lakes the *krokosis* occurred, where saffron-coloured ribbons known as *krokoi* were tied around the right hand and the left leg of each initiate. The function of the ribbons was probably apotropaic, offering protection from evil spirits.[33] The *gephyrismos* occurred at the bridge across the river Kephissos, where a group of people waited to ritually mock and harass the initiates.[34] The exact significance of this is unclear, but may have been intended to humble or possibly further rouse the communal religious fervour of the processing initiates who, regardless of being insulted, continued their advance to Eleusis.

It was night-time when the procession reached Eleusis, with flaming torches being held by initiates to guide their path. Presumably excited at their arrival, they sang and danced in honour of Demeter. Included as part of this ancient discotheque was a dance known as the *kernophoria*, performed by women carrying *kernoi* (doughnut-shaped ceramic vessels topped with multiple openings) on their heads.[35] Recalling the myth of the goddess grieving the loss of her daughter, these nocturnal festivities were an attempt to hearten Demeter. No doubt exhausted from the long day, all then dispersed to rest.

Sacrifices to Demeter were conducted on the sixth day and participants were required to fast throughout the day.[36] The period of fasting was broken with consumption of the *kykeon*, the potion of grain and herbs consumed by Demeter in her myth. The exact composition of the *kykeon* is a matter of scholarly debate, with some suggesting it contained hallucinogenic ingredients.[37] For in the next part, the climax of the ceremonies, references to the experience of initiates describe flashes of light, strange noises and apparitions. Ergot, a psychoactive fungus that grows on wheat, as well as opium and psilocybin mushrooms, have been suggested as components in the *kykeon* for their potential to produce a state of ecstasy in initiates.[38] Classical archaeologist and historian Michael Cosmopoulos points out, however, that there is little evidence for such theories. He explains the extraordinary visions in comparison to the deep religious experiences within modern Greek Orthodox Christianity:

> The darkness broken by light, which the sources mention, does not require any far-fetched explanations: anyone who has attended the solemn-turned-joyous Resurrection service of Greek Easter can testify to the depth and intensity of the experience, as the light of the Anastasi breaks the darkness of death. In the absence of any evidence for the use of entheogens, the most reasonable explanation for the use of the kykeon is also the simplest one, merely a nutritious meal with possibly calming effects, used to end the fast.[39]

During this overnight ritual the Mysteries were experienced, the most secret and sacred elements of the festival. Information at this point is therefore quite limited. The rites were conducted indoors. Initiates had their names recorded on wooden tablets as they entered this congregational building known as the Telesterion.[40] In form it resembled a hypostyle hall, a forest of columns supporting the roof of this square chamber (in contrast with the front-facing colonnade of columns that surround a more typical Classical temple). Archaeological remains from the fifth century BC indicate a temple capable of holding around 3,000 people.[41]

Of the disorientating experience of being initiated within, Sopater writes, 'I came out of the mystery hall feeling like a stranger to myself.'[42] The Mysteries witnessed inside the *Telesterion* had three components: the *dromena* ('things done'), the *legomena* ('things said') and the *deiknymena* ('things shown').[43]

The *dromena* appears to have been some kind of re-enactment, most likely the story from the Homeric Hymn to Demeter. Singing, dancing and the playing of instruments likely accompanied the performance. The Ploutonion, a cave sacred to Hades at Eleusis and regarded as an entry point to the Underworld, may have been used in dramatization of the abduction of Persephone. The sacred play was probably interactive, requiring audience participation from initiates. They took on Demeter's pain at losing her child and wandered in the darkness, imitating the search for

Photograph from a glass negative taken by William J. Woodhouse of the Telesterion, Eleusis, 1890–1935.

Persephone.[44] Plutarch, in discussing the nature of the soul, finds a comparison:

> The soul suffers as do those who have been initiated into the great Mysteries, that is why the words and the actions of dying [*teleutan*] and performing the rituals [*teleisthai*] resemble each other. At first there are wanderings and exhausting walks, and unfulfilled and unclear journeys. Before the end come all terrible things, terror and trembling and sweat and awe. But after this, a marvellous light appears, and pure spaces and meadows receive the initiate, with voices and chants and the solemnity of sacred sounds and holy spectacles.[45]

The ritual is analogous to dying, for at the point of death the soul suffers something comparable to mystery initiation. During the ritual, darkness was broken at critical points with the lighting of torches. References to blindness in texts may also indicate the use of blindfolds or hoods, which were suddenly removed at key moments.[46] The *dromena* concluded with the striking of a gong by the hierophant that announced the reunion of the goddesses.[47] The limited information we find preserved in Classical writings describes a ghostly apparition of Demeter and Persephone that appeared before the initiates. Cosmopoulos suggests this was probably a sculpture that was lit up from behind or from within.[48]

The secret words known as *legomena* that were spoken by the hierophant have not been reliably preserved. They probably provided an explanation for the symbolic events that occurred during the *dromena*. We are likewise in the dark with regard to the nature of sacred things, the *hiera* that had journeyed to Athens and back again, that were displayed to the initiates as the *deiknymena*. Emblems of Demeter and daughter, such as representations of the pomegranate or an ear of wheat, are possible candidates. The archaeologist George Mylonas suggests that they may be heirloom vessels or figurines held in continued reverence from the earlier Mycenaean culture of Greece's Bronze Age.[49] Hostile early Christian writers report the presentation of model genitalia.[50]

There was also a higher degree of initiation that returning initiates could partake in. Conducted either on the same or the following night, it has been suggested that this ritual included observing the exhibition of sacred grain and the birth of a child.[51] Those who witnessed these final revelations became *epoptai* ('beholders').

On the eighth day, the dead were honoured with libations. Participants held a vessel to the East and another to the West.[52] These were turned upside down, allowing the liquid offerings within to be received by the earth for the departed. Singing and dancing likely followed the ceremony. The festival concluded on the ninth day with initiates departing Eleusis for their homes across the Greek world. But it did not end there. A philosophical text from the fourth century BC is critical of the passivity of some initiates who

> go away after being initiated before they have understood, without asking additional questions, as though they had understood something of what they have

> seen or learned. And they must be pitied because it is not enough for them to have spent their money, but they also go off deprived of their judgement. Hoping before performing the holy rites to gain knowledge, they nevertheless go away after being initiated deprived of their expectation.[53]

For not everything would be directly explained, and contemplation would be required of the initiate if they were to comprehend what they had experienced. It would be a less confusing spectacle for those who returned to partake in the Eleusinian Mysteries a second time. Since they knew what was to come, greater understanding was gained.

The social bonds forged lasted beyond the borders of the sacred city. Together, this community had partaken in magical rites that promised humanity success in the growth of grain. Each member had developed a closer individual relationship with the goddess of agriculture. As her daughter Persephone had descended into the Underworld and was resurrected, so too they had learned secrets for both this world and the next. Though the Mysteries did not render an initiate immortal (remember that Demeter's plan for Demophoön was interrupted), death was no longer to be feared.

REPRESENTING AND MISREPRESENTING THE ELEUSINIAN MYSTERIES

There were multiple occasions when the sanctity of Eleusis was threatened and punishment exacted. Divine retribution, in the form of madness, was imposed on Spartan general

Cleomenes (*c.* 524–490 BC) for damaging the holy site during his invasion of Athens. Xerxes' (*c.* 518–465 BC) sack of Eleusis was likewise regarded by Herodotus as the reason for the later destruction of his army.[54] Livy reports that, despite their innocence, two uninitiated Acarnanian shepherds who had accidentally wandered into the sanctuary during the celebration of the secret rituals were executed in the second century BC.[55]

The most famous example, however, occurred in 415 BC. Alcibiades (*c.* 450–404 BC), an Athenian general who was soon to be leading a naval operation to Sicily, was accused of profaning the Eleusinian Mysteries.[56] He and several others were brought before a magistrate for celebrating them in a private house, divulging the secret rites to the uninitiated and making a mockery of the sacred. If the *kykeon* did include some kind of drug, this event perhaps involved recreational consumption of the hallowed beverage. Immunity was granted to an uninitiated slave who had been present. He described the Mysteries he witnessed to the room that had been cleared of all non-initiates. Alcibiades denied involvement, but ultimately looked very guilty when he fled the city. Athens passed the death sentence *in absentia*, and Alcibiades in defiance joined their Peloponnesian enemies in Sparta. Conveniently timed charges against Alcibiades may have been invented to halt the controversial Sicily Expedition. But what they illustrate for us is that sacrilege was taken very seriously. Diagoras, 'the Atheist' of Melos (fifth century BC), was similarly said to have broken a taboo by revealing secrets of the Mysteries to all:

> With reason did the Athenians adjudge Diagoras guilty of atheism, in that he not only divulged the Orphic doctrine, and published the mysteries of Eleusis and of the Cabiri, and chopped up the wooden statue of Hercules to boil his turnips, but openly declared that there was no God at all.[57]

Accused of impiety, he was banished from Athens.

Other, later sources attempted to reveal the secret rituals in the most derogatory terms. Christian apologists wrote about their apparent depravity, though none themselves had been initiates. Clement of Alexandria's *Protrepticus* provides the best example, an exhortation to the pagans of Greece to adopt Christianity. The text sought to expose the absurd practices of Eleusis as well as other mystery cults. By doing so, Clement reduces the status of the cults to harmless superstitions: 'I will convict your orgies themselves of being full of deception and jugglery, and if you have been initiated you will smile the more at these legends you are wont to honour.'[58] A bawdier version of the Eleusis myth is reported – Demeter finds relief while mourning the loss of her daughter in the amusement presented by a character who exposes their genitals to the agricultural goddess. Clement claims that the sacred objects concealed within chests were some rather ordinary cakes.

Though the aim of such Christian sources was to ridicule the Mysteries, they also unintentionally preserved details that, though distorted, have provided information on parts of the ceremonies where other texts fall silent. Clement writes of 'a mystic drama . . . that Eleusis celebrates by torchlight processions'.[59] Such night-time spectacles performed by torch light are confirmed visually on Greek pottery. The best example of this is the Ninnion Tablet, a ceramic plaque found at Eleusis that is decorated in red-figure illustration. Dated to the fourth century BC, it depicts two rows of initiates being led to Demeter and Persephone, who are seated at the right.[60] Their torch-wielding guides are Hekate and Iakkhos. The

The Ninnion Tablet. Attic red-figure naiskos-shaped plaque found at Eleusis, mid-4th century BC.

The Great Eleusinian Relief. Fragmentary Roman copy (*c.* 27 BC–AD 14) of Greek original from the 5th century BC.

scene depicts motifs emblematic of the Mysteries, including wreaths of myrtle, *kernoi* upon the heads of the female initiates and the *cista* chest that conceals the *hiera*. A dedicatory inscription inscribed on the bottom indicates that it was offered by a woman named Ninnion, who is perhaps one of the participants depicted on the tablet.

Another frequently encountered Eleusinian image to appear on Greek vases is that of Triptolemus upon his winged and snaky chariot. He commonly wears a myrtle wreath on his head, holding stalks of wheat and a staff in one hand with a phiale libation bowl in the other. One or both Eleusinian goddesses are usually depicted sending him off with flaming torches, alluding to the nocturne rites of the Mysteries. Sophocles wrote a lost play bearing the hero's name. Fragments of *Triptolemus* do survive, one of which hints at the afterlife benefits conferred on initiates of Eleusis: 'Thrice blessed are those mortals who have seen these rites and thus enter into Hades: for them alone there is life, for the others all is misery.'[61] The plot of the tragedy is unknown but likely centred on spreading the art of agriculture, the departure for this mission being the subject of these red-figure vases. Triptolemus' journey is symbolic of that of the initiate as they leave Eleusis filled with sacred knowledge. Triptolemus is also depicted on the Great Eleusinian Relief, rendered as a young naked boy with Demeter and Persephone flanking either side of him. It was found at Eleusis, where it was used in the Byzantine period as a threshold of a church. This marble relief that dates from the fifth century BC also survives in Roman copies.[62] Demeter stands on the left, holding a sceptre. She hands something to Triptolemus. This is most likely her sacred ear of grain, which does not survive in the relief and was probably made of bronze. Persephone, on the right, wields a flaming torch and blesses the boy.

THE OTHER MYSTERIES OF DEMETER

There were several smaller, derivative local mystery religions that celebrated Demeter and her daughter. Though related to Eleusis, each had its own unique practices. In an example based at Pheneos, the focus was on a structure known as the Petroma that consisted of two large stones fitted together.[63] It was used for the swearing of oaths. Within the Petroma were stored ritual texts that were only withdrawn to be read aloud to initiates, and then returned on the same night. It also housed a mask of Demeter that was put on by a priest during the Mysteries.

Pausanias reports that the Andanian Mysteries, which were practised in the Peloponnese, were first brought to Messenia from Eleusis.[64] They apparently fell into disuse, but were revived in 360 BC when a local military hero had a dream that led him to unearth a bronze vessel. It contained a scroll made of tin that described the secret rituals. Our understanding of the Andanian Mysteries of Messina is otherwise principally from a long inscription of 91 BC that lays out the regulations for conduct of the rites.[65] In the document we find strong emphasis on the appropriate clothing required for various classes of both male and female initiates. The personnel necessary for a great procession are recorded. These included a pageant of women who were 'dressed in the manner of the gods' and musicians ('as many capable performers on the flute and lyre as they may find').[66] Carts carried chests containing the sacred objects of the Mysteries. Sacrificial animals accompanied the parade. Other practicalities were also accounted for, including tents for housing attendees, a market to provide them with food and bathing provisions, as well as access to drinking water and firewood. As Hugh Bowden succinctly states, 'The whole event has the air of an outdoor weekend music festival.'[67] After the public aspects were performed, the initiated were taken to witness the Mysteries in a sacred grove.

Curiouser still are the Mysteries of Despoina. Pausanias reports a particularly unusual, and rather frenzied, form of sacrifice practised in the cult: 'they do not cut the throats of the victims, as is done in other sacrifices; each person chops off a limb of the sacrifice, whichever happens to come to hand.'[68] Despoina was venerated in Arcadia, principally at a site called Lycosura, where a mythology particular to the region developed around Demeter. The Arcadian version reports that while searching for Persephone, Demeter is pursued by the god of the sea, Poseidon (Neptune). She transforms herself into a mare in an attempt to evade his advances. But, taking the form of a stallion, Poseidon nonetheless rapes her. Having lost a child and now been sexually assaulted, Demeter dresses herself in black clothes of mourning and withdraws into a cave. For this reason, the goddess was given an epithet specific in Arcadia: Black (*Melaina*) Demeter. The encounter results in the birth of a divine horse named Arion and a second daughter who was venerated by the title Despoina, which simply means 'Mistress'. The true name of the goddess eludes us today,[69] as it was guarded with secrecy

Moulded terracotta plaque from Locri depicting
Hades and Persephone enthroned, 5th century BC.

and only revealed to those initiated in her Mysteries. Sacred laws prohibited women who were pregnant or breastfeeding from entering Despoina's sanctuary, probably in connection with the strange story of her birth.[70]

Despoina was closely affiliated with animals. A sacred deer was her companion. Pausanias reports Mount Elaius to be the locale for the cave of Demeter's retreat and describes a (now lost) theriomorphic wooden cult statue there:

> It was seated on a rock, like to a woman in all respects save the head. She had the head and hair of a horse, and there grew out of her head images of serpents and other beasts. Her tunic reached right to her feet; on one of her hands was a dolphin, on the other a dove.[71]

Animal-headed figures are found elsewhere in connection with Despoina's cult. Fragments of the marble cult statues of Despoina and Demeter have been discovered during archaeological excavation of the temple at Lycosura. The himation worn by Despoina is sculptured with elaborate bands of decoration: eagles flying alongside thunderbolts, winged Nike figures holding incense burners, Nereids riding marine creatures. Most interesting of all is the register of the human figures with various animal heads (likely masks used in the Mystery rituals) that dance and play musical instruments. More than one hundred terracotta animal-headed figurines that were left as offerings to Despoina within the sanctuary at Lycosura have also been found.[72]

Being the most revered cult in antiquity, Eleusis provides a good basis for understanding the rites we will examine in subsequent chapters. The influence of Demeter's Mysteries is clear in the derivative practices of many of these. Persephone, in her role as Queen of the Underworld, also came to play a key role in several of these traditions. But we must move on, as now it is time to be initiated into our next cult.

Small bronze bust of Isis from Roman Egypt, AD 60–270. The goddess wears a horned sun-disc and her garment is tied at the breast in an Isis knot. Two pierced holes were used to afix the image to something.

THREE

GRECO-ROMAN EGYPTOMANIA: ISIS AND SERAPIS

To Greeks and Romans, the Nile Valley was exotic and magical, an image that has persisted into the modern age. They viewed Egypt as a source of ancient wisdom. The mysteries of the goddess Isis saw aspects from Egyptian religion being exported abroad to the Classical world. The cult developed during the era when Egypt was under the Macedonian rule of the Ptolemies. Most evidence for her religious following, however, comes from the Roman Empire, when the cult of Isis was at its height. A goddess who resurrected her husband Osiris from death, Isis appealed in her potential to offer initiates exclusive entry into a blissful afterlife. There is a departure from the type of Mysteries practised at Eleusis in that *mystes* was not used in reference to those who had witnessed secret rituals of induction. There was also an expectation of continued ritual participation and service in the cult following initiation.[1] There appear to have been multiple levels of revelation, and attainment of each allowed an individual to advance in the cult hierarchy.

FROM EGYPTIAN GODDESS TO GRECO-ROMAN DEITY

The ancient Egyptians had long held Isis in reverence, with the earliest references to the goddess found in Old Kingdom texts of the third millennium BC.[2] The fundamental myth of Isis and her husband Osiris had its origin during this period. The story was widespread in Egypt, with elements of the narrative referenced in funerary, temple and magical texts right up until the Classical era. No Egyptian source gives a full narration of the myth and therefore Plutarch's account of the first century AD (which also reflects understanding of the goddess' Classical mysteries) has come to be the most popularly known version of the story.[3] Egyptian reluctance appears to have prevented portraying certain aspects of the story. They alluded to, but never clearly described, the murder of Osiris in the myth.

Osiris is King of Egypt, regarded as the first Pharaoh, ruling alongside his sister-wife Isis. His younger brother Seth, a god of storms, the desert and chaos, is jealous of his prosperity. Seth plots against Osiris, intent on murdering him and taking the throne of Egypt. At the climax of a great feast held by Seth, the god reveals a beautifully decorated chest. He offers this prize to anyone who can fit inside. Having specifically crafted it to Osiris' dimensions, Seth convinces his elder brother to get into the box. Seth slams the lid down and seals Osiris in the container that becomes his coffin. The funereal vessel is then thrown into the Nile and carried down the river. Isis mourns the death of her husband and eventually retrieves the body with the intention of restoring

Osiris to life. Seth, unwilling to let this happen, steals and dismembers the corpse, scattering the pieces across Egypt.

Isis wanders the land, seeking out each fragment and building a temple of Osiris at each location she finds a piece of his divine body. One critical part of the dead king's body remained missing, his penis, which has been consumed by the Medjed elephantfish (this species apparently being ever after forbidden from human consumption). Isis therefore uses her magic to fashion him a new member and then revives Osiris through the process of mummification. Having copulated with her resurrected husband, she then gives birth to a son named Horus. Horus fights Seth in a mighty battle and defeats the usurper. Order is restored to Egypt, with Horus installed as king and Osiris descending to the Underworld to judge the souls of the dead. The land remained dependant on the generative powers of Osiris that influenced the annual flooding of the Nile and fertility of crops. The divine father and son came to be reflected in Egyptian ideology of kingship: a living pharaoh was identified with Horus and was believed to become Osiris in death.[4] This gave Isis a special relationship (being mother, wife and sister) to the pharaoh.

Elements familiar from Greco-Roman mysteries were already present in Egyptian reverence of Osiris. An annual festival was held in honour of the god at his cult centre of Abydos. Scenes from the myth were ritually re-enacted during the public festivities. Purification rituals enacted prior to the climactic staging of Osiris' resurrection, however, were conducted in secret by a restricted audience of senior religious officials inside a building.[5] The major temple to Osiris

Fresco from Pompeii depicting a priest wearing a mask of Anubis.

at Abydos was decorated around 1300 BC with bas-reliefs and painted scenes that depict parts of the festival and myth. The images illustrate the gods with their typical Egyptian iconography: falcon-headed Horus, Isis with a throne-shaped hieroglyph on her head and Osiris as a mummy wrapped in linen. The first temple of Isis to be built in Greece dates from the fourth century BC, constructed by Egyptians living in Athens who acquired land to use for her sanctuary.[6] This is one of the earliest temples dedicated specifically to the goddess. Temples to Isis were first constructed in Egypt around the same time (most notably on Philae Island). For while Isis had long been revered by the Egyptians, it had been within temples of her husband. The impetus for this seems to have been a resurgence of Egyptian nationalism during the short-lived period of independence from Persian rule under the (last) native Egyptian pharaohs of the Thirtieth Dynasty.[7]

Other Egyptian deities were adopted with Isis by the Classical world in the imagery and ritual associated with her Mysteries. Such was the case for Anubis, the god of mummification. A fresco from the Temple of Isis in Pompeii depicts a priest dressed as the jackal-headed god in Roman attire. Sometimes he was syncretized with Hermes, whose role in the Underworld as Psychopompos saw the two gods combined in the form of Hermanubis, a jackal-headed god who holds the *caduceus*. Other deities were rendered completely new. While Horus in traditional Egyptian religion was a sky-god, the Classical world rebranded the son of Osiris and Isis as Harpocrates. Associated with silence and secrets, he is usually depicted as an infant with a finger held towards his

Roman marble statue of Hermanubis, 2nd century AD.
The jackal-headed god has a small horned sun-disc between his ears and holds the caduceus.

Fig wood panel painted with image of Serapis, AD 100–200. It originally functioned as the left door of a small devotional shrine, with the surviving right-hand door depicting Isis. His golden kantharos crown is covered with ivy branches, and further vegetation emanates from his head.

lips in a hushing gesture. Horus/Harpocrates often appears in iconography being nursed on the lap of Isis. Even more interesting is the god Serapis, a conglomeration of aspects of multiple Egyptian and Greek gods first promoted by Ptolemy I as a unifying force for the mixed population living in Hellenistic Egypt. In Serapis, elements of the Egyptian gods Osiris and Apis were syncretized with the Greek gods Hades, Asclepius and Dionysus.[8] His easily recognizable iconography depicts the god as a bearded man with a *kalathos* (also referred to as a *modius*) grain measure atop his head. Often vegetation sprouts up the sides of the

Roman marble statues depicting Isis (who is syncretized here with Persephone) and Serapis (with attributes of Hades).

vessel. Sometimes at his feet sits the three-headed dog Kerberos, who guarded the god's domain in the Underworld. In Classical Isis worship, Osiris came to be replaced by Serapis as her spouse.

Isis in the Classical world was often compared with Demeter, her rites modelled on the Eleusinian Mysteries. Both searched for and saw the restoration of a loved one taken by death. Isis was a multifaceted goddess, regarded as having particular sway over the domains of motherhood, magic, fertility, healing and seafaring. Her association with the Egyptian harvest was particularly important for the Romans, who depended on Egypt as a supplier of grain. The many powers of Isis are evoked in a body of ritual literature known as aretalogies. This type of text was written from the perspective of a deity who lists their attributes and accomplishments. The aretalogy of Isis from Cyme gives the impression that there is nothing in the correct ordering of the universe for which she isn't responsible:

> I divided the earth from the heaven.
> I showed the paths of the stars
> I ordered the courses of the sun and the moon . . .
>
> I revealed mysteries unto men.
> I taught men to honour images of the gods.
> I consecrated the precincts of the gods . . .
>
> I am the Queen of war.
> I am the Queen of the thunderbolt.
> I stir up the sea and I calm it.[9]

The multitasking goddess praises herself for having invented writing, brought an end to human cannibalism, built the first city walls and contrived love between partners. As a lawgiver, she ensures that the wicked do not prosper. Objects used in the Isiac Mysteries were both imported from Egypt and created locally (with imitations often rather superficially rendered) in Egyptian style. Cultic art and rituals were thus a unique blend of Egyptian and Greco-Roman elements. Several temples of Isis, such as that at Pompeii, had pools that were apparently filled with sacred Nile water (or at least perceived to be), used in purification ceremonies of the cult.[10] The performance of a water ceremony is found on a fresco from Herculaneum. A priest holds up a vessel of sacred water at the door of a temple flanked by sphinxes and palm trees. A second priest tends a fire flanked by

Temple of Isis at Pompeii.

Fresco depicting an Isiac ceremony from Herculaneum.

worshippers who play musical instruments or raise their hands in adoration. Egypt is further evoked with ibises who stalk the foreground.

Ritual ablutions prescribed shaving of the head for male devotees.[11] An exceptional depiction of a male worshipper is the Ptolemaic priest of Isis rendered in black granite recovered in an underwater archaeology expedition conducted in the harbour of Alexandria (and thus heavily weathered). His head is shaved and his hands concealed beneath the folds of his cloak. He reverently holds up an Osiris-headed jar. In the formative period of the cult, Egyptians were brought to

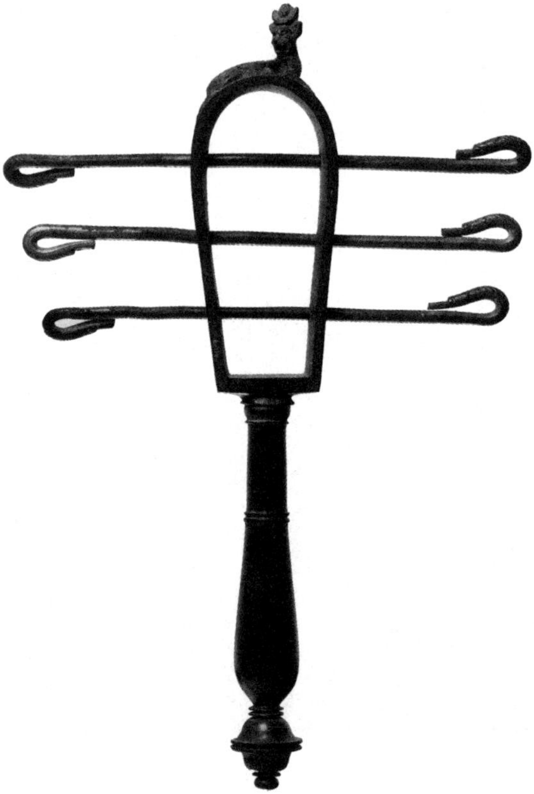

Bronze sistrum, 1st–2nd century AD.

Greece to perform as priests in temples to Isis and Serapis. Initially priesthood for the divine couple was reserved for men.[12] By the time of the Roman Empire, however, priestesses were major figures in the cult, as Isis had ascended to become the more important of the two gods.

Symbols associated with Isis worship included the *sistrum*, a rattle used in Egyptian ceremonies, and the *situla*, a pail used for carrying the Nilotic water used in these rites. Female devotees are identifiable in Classical sculpture by the holding of these attributes, as well as a tie across the front of their

Terracotta votive of Isis-Aphrodite, 332–330 BC. She wears an elaborate headress emblazoned with a small horned-disc. The goddess lifts her robe to expose her genitals, the fabric billowing behind her.

Small terracotta sculpture of Isis-Thermouthis, 2nd century AD.

draped garments known as the Isis knot. Images of the goddess likewise depict her in Classical drapery with the knot and holding a sistrum, her brow crowned with the Egyptian motif of a sun-disc between a pair of cow horns. Sometimes Isis was syncretized with other deities in the creation of composite gods with combined powers. This is the case for many terracotta votives known to represent Isis-Aphrodite. In this fertility-rich aspect of the goddess, she is naked or suggestively lifts her robe to reveal her genitals (a gesture known as *anasyrma*).[13] The large, elaborate *kalathos* crown (decorated with a tiny horned-disc motif) that Isis-Aphrodite wears amplifies the effect of her nudity. Another common type was Isis-Fortuna, who holds a cornucopia and the rudder of a ship. The agricultural variant Isis-Thermouthis had the torso of a woman with the lower body of a snake.

FESTIVALS AND CULT PRACTICE

Although essential elements were shared by different communities of Isis worshippers, there were local variations of the cult and not all her temples practised mystery initiations. An unusual form of sacrifice is described by Pausanias that occurred at a biannual festival of Isis in Tithorea, Phocis.[14] Instead of burning a sacrificial animal, once killed it was wrapped in linen. The offering was then deposited in a sunken room for the goddess and left there to rot, removed the day before the next festival. Underground chambers at other temples to Isis may have been used in initiation. It has been suggested that in such a crypt excavated at Gortyn on Crete, initiates were required to spend a period

of confinement that imitated Osiris being locked in the chest.[15] Many people's relationships to the goddess, however, would not have involved such mystic rites. Rather, they were confined to the experience of public annual festivals held in honour of Isis.

The *Navigium Isidis* was a celebration of the influence Isis held over the sea that was conducted each year in March.[16] It augurated the new sailing season, recalling the journey down the Nile taken by Isis in search of Osiris. The festivities were performed in multiple locations, with a procession beginning at the local Isis temple that moved towards the harbour. The parade featured members of the priesthood and Isiac devotees who carried sacred objects, with emphasis on a model ship that was launched in the water. In the city of Rome for instance, the ceremonial boat was carried from the Iseum Campense temple on the Campus Martius and set afloat in the Tiber. An eyewitness account captures the festivity of the *Navigium Isidis*:

> The chief priest consecrated a ship, which was constructed with fine craftsmanship and decorated all over with marvellous Egyptian pictures. He took a lighted torch, an egg, and sulphur, uttered prayers of great solemnity and reverent lips, and purified the ship thoroughly, naming it and dedicating it to the goddess. The gleaming sail of this holy barque bore

Marble funerary monument from the Athenian Keremeikos cemetery for a priestess of Isis named Alexandra, 2nd century AD. She holds a situla in one hand and it is likely she wielded a sistrum in the other. Her garment is tied with the Isis knot at the front.

> an inscription woven in letters of gold, whose text renewed the prayer for prosperous navigation . . . Then all the people, worshippers and uninitiated alike, outdid one another in loading the ship with baskets heaped with spices and similar offerings, and on the waves they poured libations of grain-mash made with milk. When the ship was laden with generous gifts and auspicious sacrifices, it was untied from its anchor-ropes and offered to the sea, as a mild breeze rose specially for her.[17]

The crowd then dispersed, with only the priesthood and those initiated returning to the temple to replace the sacred images used in the pageant. The event was particularly relevant for sailors, merchants and upcoming travellers as the rites promised safe and prosperous voyage for the coming months.

There is evidence that beds may have played an important role in cult practice, possibly as part of a symbolic resurrection of Osiris or of his marriage to Isis. A funerary inscription of a certain Meniketes from Bithynia relates that he had furnished beds for use by Isis that were 'forbidden to the laymen'.[18] Meniketes asserts that because he made this ritual furniture during life, in death he is 'hastened to the harbors of the Blessed'. A passage in Josephus (AD 37–100) relates an anecdote concerning a woman who was summoned to the temple of Isis in Rome to dine and share a bed with the god Anubis.[19] The scandal of AD 19 centred on a reputable married woman named Paulina. She was loved by another man named Decius Mundus. Despite repeated appeals and gifts,

Fresco from Pompeii depicting an individual making an offering before the enshrined sarcophagus of Osiris. Another man stands fishing in the river that surrounds the sanctuary.

Paulina was a virtuous woman who would not be unfaithful to her husband. She was also a devotee of Isis. A plan was devised in which priests of the goddess were bribed to tell Paulina that the god Anubis had requested to spend the night with her in the Isiac sanctuary. Honoured at the invitation, she tells friends and even her husband who, with no doubt as to her fidelity, allows her to go and meet the deity. The shrine is locked by the priests, the lamps extinguished. In the darkness, Mundus adopts the persona of Anubis. Under the belief that she was providing service to the god, she has sex with him. Mundus later boasts to Paulina of his successful scheme. Appalled, she has her husband bring the matter to the attention of the emperor, Tiberius. In response, Mundus is exiled, the priests are crucified, the temple is demolished and the statue of Isis is thrown into the Tiber River. It's possible that this story preserves truth concerning Isiac bed rituals, but in an exaggerated manner. For rituals that are surrounded with secrecy are open to misinterpretation and slanderous rumour.

APULEIUS AND THE GOLDEN ASS

The quotation above describing the *Navigium Isidis* comes from the major literary source on the Mysteries of Isis, a novel written by Apuleius (second century AD) known as *The Metamorphoses* or *The Golden Ass*. It narrates the comical adventures of a Corinthian man named Lucius, who is accidentally transformed into a donkey as a result of his foolish curiosity about magic. Throughout the tale, several independent short stories (notably the myth of Cupid and Psyche) are interwoven into the main narrative – these being narrated by various characters. The humorous tone of the novel, however, shifts into one of reverence in Book XI of the text, when Isis herself appears before Lucius in a dream. Dreams played an important role in the cult of Isis and there is evidence of some temples practising incubation in the hope that an individual would receive a divine message while sleeping within.[20] Pausanias reports that only those who had been summoned directly by Isis in a dream were permitted to enter her temple in Tithorea, Phocis.[21] In his vision of the goddess on a beach, Lucius is instructed as to how he can restore his human form by eating some roses at a religious procession held in her honour the next day. With his hominoid body back, he is then initiated into her Mysteries.

To be initiated requires payment by Lucius, a period of fasting and sexual abstinence. He makes ablutions at the local baths and a priest asks the gods to forgive any previous wrongdoings of Lucius as part of this purification process. These aspects of the novel reflect the author's own experience, Apuleius having been initiated into the Cult of Isis (as well as many other Mystery religions).[22] He describes priests reading from texts written in a script that we can recognize as being Egyptian hieroglyphics:

Fresco from Pompeii depicting a mythological scene in which Io (sporting cow horns and carried upon a personification of the river Nile) is welcomed into Egypt by Isis. Worshippers of the goddess stand behind their patron wielding instruments of her cult – the sistrum and situla.

> Some used the shapes of all sorts of animals to represent abridged expressions of liturgical language; in others ends of the letters were knotted and curved like wheels or interwoven like vine-tendrils to protect their meaning from the curiosity of the uninitiated.[23]

Once Lucius is ready, he is dressed in a new linen robe and taken at night to an underground vault within the temple of Isis. Although Apuleius states he will not describe what happened within, he nonetheless gives an awe-inspiring vision of this climactic moment of initiation:

> I approached the frontier of death, I set foot on the threshold of Persephone, I journeyed through all the elements and came back, I saw at midnight the sun, sparkling in white light, I came close to the gods of the upper and nether world and adored them from near at hand.[24]

The Underworld descent of the initiate showcases the power of Isis over life and death. Boundaries between worlds are broken and closeness of the initiate to the gods is emphasized. The reference to solar illumination that lights up the night has been compared with imagery from the ancient Egyptian *Book of the Dead* of the nocturne sun as it passes through the Underworld.[25] While this funerary text had ceased being copied by this time, elements of such symbolism found continuity in oral tradition of the Egyptian priesthood.

Lucius emerges from the chamber the next morning triumphantly reborn and dressed in a sumptuous twelve-layer garment (symbolizing either the zodiac or the twelve hours of night passed in the Underworld).[26] He resembles the sun god Helios, wielding a flaming torch and wearing a solar crown of radiating palm fronds. Before a crowd of worshippers, he ascends a platform in the centre of the temple to

Marble bust of Antinous, *c.* AD 130.

stand next to the elevated cult statue of Isis. Days of feasting follow. Though he returns to his home of Corinth, the goddess then requires Lucius to relocate to Rome. A year passes before Lucius is informed that he must undergo a second initiation. Shortly after this, he is apparently due for a third. The wit of Apuleius is evident in the doubts of sincerity that the protagonist expresses at the repeated costs demanded for each level of revelation. Yet at the conclusion of the novel Lucius has been appointed to a high position within the priesthood of Isis, and her divine favour has enabled him to receive a steady income as a lawyer. Having undergone what is described as a 'voluntary death', when Lucius actually dies, he will have the perception to see Isis shining in the darkness of the Underworld and worship her there.[27]

The Roman world also saw the spread of the Egyptian-inspired cult of Antinous. The experience of the young lover of Hadrian, who in AD 130 drowned in the river Nile and was subsequently deified, was identified with that of Osiris.[28] The heartbroken emperor, in parallel with the grieving Isis, had Antinous embalmed and mummified by priests in Egypt. Temples and smaller shrines dedicated to Antinous were constructed across the empire. The city of Antinoöpolis was founded close to his place of death. Statues depicting Antinous as a heroic nude became widespread, and sometimes represent him as wearing the pharaonic *nemes* headdress. Pausanias records that in at least one location, Mantineia in Arcadia, mystery rites were included in worship of the youth.[29] But Egypt was not the only source for Eastern-styled initiations. The god of our next chapter derived from Iranian origins.

FOUR

MITHRAISM: A BOYS' CLUB

The cult of Mithras was widespread across the Roman world from the first to the fourth century AD.[1] It was thus a relatively late arrival in Roman religion. The deity at the centre of this mystery religion bears very little in common with his namesake Zoroastrian god Mitra of Persia. The earliest reference to Mitra is in a fourteenth-century BC document from the Hittite capital of Hattusa, where he is evoked as one of the divine guarantors of a treaty.[2] In the Persian collection of religious texts known as the *Avesta* he is praised as a god of light and truth, his name meaning contract, agreement or friend.[3] There have been attempts in the past to reconstruct the Roman cult of Mithras as a transplant of Zoroastrianism within Roman religion.[4] While there was some adoption of Persian imagery, the Roman Mithras developed from Classical perceptions of Iranian ideas. The Persian phrase *nama* ('hail') was likewise adopted as an honorific greeting directed both at the god and between the initiated.[5]

Mithraism was particularly popular among soldiers of the Roman army, and worship of the god was scattered to the frontiers of the empire. Evidence of the cult is found in more than four hundred locations.[6] The subterranean space for conducting rites to Mithras, known as a Mithraeum, was constructed as either an artificial or modified natural cave.[7] These dark, windowless spaces would have been illuminated by lamp and torchlight. Each of these Mithraea was roughly rectangular in form with a barrel-vaulted ceiling. They are small and congregational temples, each with a capacity of twenty to fifty people.[8] A single locality could have multiple Mithraea. The city of Ostia, for example, has seventeen known examples.[9] People were seated or reclined on benches running down both the long sides of the central room, with focus of worship on a cult image of Mithras at the end opposite the entrance. Additional marble statues and altars were also part of the decorative programme. Bells found in several Mithraea attest to the ceremonial music that once echoed through these rather cramped spaces.[10] Walls were usually painted, with the floor of the central aisle often

The tauroctony in the mithraeum of Capua, 2nd century AD, is painted as a fresco on the back wall.

Freestanding marble sculpture of the tauroctony (bull-slaying) by Mithras, 2nd century AD.

decorated in mosaic. Side rooms were used for storage and the preparation of food used in rituals.

Astronomical imagery was used throughout the Mithraeum, decorated with stars and planets to recreate the universe in microcosm. The Neoplatonist writer Porphyry (third century AD) states, 'Zoroaster was the first to dedicate a cave to Mithras, the creator and father of all, since the cave was for him the image of the universe created by Mithras, and the inner arrangements inside the cave were signs of the elements and zones of the world.'[11] The space both evoked the celestial sphere and replicated the cave where Mithras had sacrificed an astrological bull in myth. The cult appealed to initiates for the exclusive knowledge it provided them on their place in the universe, epitomized in the cosmic layout of these temples and the rituals conducted within.

IMAGERY OF MITHRAS

While no mythological narratives survive in written records of the cult, the myths of Mithras are evoked in imagery produced for his cult. Fundamental to the temple was the central icon known as the tauroctony, which depicts Mithras killing a bull within a cave. Illustrations of the lead-up indicate a lively pursuit, capture, escape and recapture of the animal prior to this key moment. From where the bull came is unclear, with Christian sources referring to Mithras as a common cattle thief.[12] The bull, with its crescent-shaped horns, is a lunar symbol in the Classical world and it may be that the beast was fetched from the pastures of the Moon.[13] Though there are some minor variations, the tauroctony is highly uniform. Mithras is illustrated at its centre wearing the oriental attire of a Phrygian cap (characteristically soft and conical with its tip flopped forwards) and a tunic with a billowing cloak. The god is positioned with one knee pressed down on the back of a bull. His other leg is almost fully extended as it restrains the bovine rump and hind leg. With one hand, the god pulls back the bull's head. His other hand wields either a knife or dagger, which is plunged into the neck of the animal. A serpent and a dog reach up to drink the blood that pours from the wound. This blood is sometimes represented morphing into a bunch of grapes. Below, a scorpion bites the bull's testicles. The tail of the bull often terminates as an ear of wheat. Busts of Sol and Luna float on either side above the scene. More occasionally, these personifications of the Sun and the Moon are depicted driving their ethereal chariots across the heavens. Joining them in the sky is a bird that has been identified as a raven. Flanking the sacrifice are Cautes and Cautopates, the two torch-bearing attendants of Mithras.[14] The pair are dressed similarly to Mithras in the perceived 'Eastern' attire of Phrygian cap and tunic, though on smaller scale to the god. Cautes holds his torch raised up, while Cautopates points his downward with the flame inverted. The brothers have been interpreted as representing sunrise and sunset

Stone slab with low-relief decoration
depicting the tauroctony, 2nd–3rd century AD.

Marble statue of Cautes with his torch raised, 3rd century AD.
Marble statue of Cautopates with his torch pointing downwards, 3rd century AD.

or perhaps the two equinoxes. Depictions of the tauroctony from the Rhine-Danube region include the additional elements of a cup and lion below the bull.[15] The recurring image was the focus of worship for each Mithraea as a free-standing sculptural group, carved in relief or a painted fresco on the back wall.

While most ancient cult statues represent an exalted deity either seated or standing, the tauroctony is atypical in its depiction of a god in action. The scene is highly symbolic and there is no consensus on how it should be interpreted.

The most common scholarly reading of the imagery sees the various elements together as an astronomical map.[16] The bull is Taurus and the scorpion is Scorpio. Between these two constellations is a region of the night sky that is visible at the height of summer in the northern hemisphere. There are references in the tauroctony to the constellations that appear in this narrow band of sky: Canis Major/Minor (the dog), Hydra (the snake), Gemini (Cautes and Cautopates), Corvus (the raven), Crater (the cup), Leo (the lion) and Virgo (its star Spica being an ear of wheat). The astrological significance is made even more apparent in several examples that feature a circle/band of the twelve zodiac signs or the personified planets surrounding the scene. The tauroctony contributes to making each Mithraeum a microcosmic representation of the universe. It is also an image of transformation: the scorpion, dog and snake readily latch upon the dying animal to absorb some of its potent life force.[17] The bull's tail is transfigured into grain, the staple food of humanity. The slaying of the bull is an act of creation by Mithras, who is a saviour god to his initiates. The tauroctony was likely the nucleus for the retelling of a lost myth about Mithras that was only shared with initiates sitting in the dark temple, their eyes transfixed on the torchlit image. Some reliefs (known as *amphigylphs*) depicting the tauroctony are double-sided, with other scenes from the life of Mithras on the reverse. They were designed to be rotated on a pivot at a key ceremonial moment. The entire scene or parts of the image may also have been covered and progressively unveiled.[18] Perhaps more of the icon's significance was revealed with each level of initiation.

Following his slaughter of the bull, another common scene depicted in Mithraic temples illustrates the aftermath. Mithras meets the sun god Sol, the pair greeting each other with a handshake. This is an interesting union of two manifestations of a single concept, as Mithras is also a solar deity whose full title is *Deus Sol Invictus Mithras* – 'The Unconquered Sun God Mithras'.[19] Historian Manfred Clauss best sums up the paradoxical nature of their relationship: 'Mithras is Sol, and at the same time Sol is Mithras' companion.'[20] The

High-relief sculpture group of Mithras slaying the bull flanked by the torchbearers. The chariots of the Sun and the Moon soar across the sky above the cave. From the Capitoline Hill, 2nd century AD.

clasping of arms denotes a close bond of friendship between the pair. On a table covered with the bovine hide (or sometimes simply atop the dead animal), Sol and Mithras then share a meal. With the ascent of the Sun, the Moon is overcome, as symbolized by domination of the bull.[21] Mithras and Sol banquet on loaves of bread, cups of wine and skewers of meat. This reflects cult practice, feasting evident in the archaeological record of Mithraea. Evidence of a huge feast attended by between one hundred and three hundred people is apparent in remains found in a pit beside the small Tienen Mithraeum in Belgium.[22] This deposit is from a single occasion held at the end of June or early July, possibly to celebrate the summer solstice. The sacrificial remains include 285 cockerels, ten piglets, fourteen lambs, two eels, a jackdaw and a hare. Other than the eels (whose gender is hard to distinguish), all of these animals were male and the majority were juvenile. Also note the lack of beef, a reflection that the first sacrifice performed by Mithras was an inimitable act.[23] Deliberate smashing of the vessels used in the feast followed the event. These included more than 100 incense burners, 85 dishes, 80 cooking jars and 79 drinking vessels.[24] Among the debris was a unique wine jar featuring a relief decoration of a snake wrapped around the vessel. This was connected to a pipe within the jar. When sealed and heated over a flame, wine from inside the vessel would spit from the serpent's mouth. This may be an allusion to the blood-drinking serpent of the tauroctony.[25] It is impossible to know whether it was used for a specific cult ritual, but it does reflect the type of spectacle used by mystery religions for creating atmosphere.

Fresco of Sol and Mithras reclining to share a meal.
From Mithraeum at Dura-Europos, Syria, *c.* AD 210.

The sharing of smaller, regular meals is evident from more modest remnants of eating and drinking found inside other Mithraea. Some of the surviving red-ware pottery used in the cult featured moulded decoration depicting the tauroctony and other Mithraic images. Other vessels were inscribed with text dedicating them to the god. Writing on vases offered by a certain Tertius, son of Rusticus, noted his dedication of ten such vessels to Mithras (two of which have been found).[26] Most ceramics, however, were plain, or decorated with stock motifs common in moulded Roman red-ware. Such Mithraic dining deviated from standard civic religion in its consumption of victuals *within* the temple of the god. The sharing of the communal meal was especially important as a way of affirming social bonds between initiates, as no major public festivals were conducted in honour of Mithras.[27] In the mythological image of the god seated to dine that was repeated in each Mithraeum, he becomes the host of the meal that he shares with his initiates.

Other mythological representations flesh out Mithras' story further. The god appears to have been born from a rock. A variation has the god born from an egg. Sculptures depict Mithras emerging as a fully formed naked youth (although already wearing the Phrygian cap) from a jagged stone mound, holding a dagger in one hand and a flaming torch in the other. Rising out of the earth, he brings forth light – apparently on 25 December, the date associated with his birthday.[28] Cautes and Cautopates are frequently depicted as witnesses of the miraculous birth, with the pair assisting by pulling his arms in one representation from Ptuj.[29] The most curious example of the rock birth is from a silver denarius that has been reworked into a talisman.[30] It was found at St Albans in England. This coin is of a type from 19 BC depicting a legendary episode from Rome's early history. It was struck with the motif of Tarpeia with her arms raised, as she is crushed to death beneath a pile of shields. This was the punishment allotted to her for having betrayed Rome to the Sabines in exchange for jewellery.[31] The coin was modified later, its worn-down image of Tarpeia transformed into an outline of Mithras emerging from the rock. The inscribed legend has been filed off, with the head of the emperor Augustus on the reverse completely removed and replaced with the name of Mithras.[32] Found in an archaeological layer of the second century AD, the coin took on a new identity as a devotional token some two hundred years after it was struck.

PETRAM·GENETRICEM·
AVR BASSINVS AEDITVVS
PRINCIPIORVM CAST·PER EC·
DEDICAVIT·HOC·IN·ID·CO·ET·D·D
ANTISTIANIE·A·CAEDICIO
PRISCIANO·EQ·R·PATRE

Another recurring scene from his life depicts Mithras performing a water miracle in which he creates a spring.[33] The god is represented seated, flexing a bow to fire an arrow at a rock. A second individual kneels waiting in anticipation with cupped hands ready to catch the stream that will issue forth. Water played an important role in the cult, with Mithraea commonly located close by springs or streams. At one of these in Poetovio, an altar was set up that refers to Mithras as *fons perennis*, an ever-flowing spring.[34] The Christian writer Tertullian (*c.* AD 155–220) refers to Mithras marking or sealing his followers on the forehead, this likely being a reference to some sort of purification ritual using water or oil.[35] An additional repeated image found in multiple Mithraea depicts the god approaching a tree or emerging from among its branches. He appears to be intent on plucking fruit from the plant. This takes on a fantastic quality in its depictions at Rückingen and Dieburg where the tree has three branches that each terminate in a head crowned with a Phrygian cap.[36] A final scene of his adventures depicts Mithras joining Sol in his chariot, possibly a victorious ascent for the god into the heavens.

Aside from these narrative exploits, a curious associate of Mithras is the Leontocephaline figure, who also appears in relief and sculpture found at multiple Mithraea. This lion-headed god has the body of a naked man around which is coiled a serpent. Feathered wings sprout from his back. He frequently holds keys and a sceptre. Astrological symbols or a thunderbolt are sometimes carved upon the flesh of his

Marble statue depicting Mithras being born from the rock, torch and dagger in hand. Dedicated by a certain Aurelius Bassinus, 2nd century AD.

Stone relief depicting a tree with three branches terminating in heads wearing Phrygian caps, from Mithraeum at Dieburg, 2nd–3rd century AD.

torso. Fire-breathing appears to be one of this god's attributes. In a relief from Rome the Leontocephaline kindles flames upon an altar with his breath.[37] A marble sculpture of the god from the Mithraeum in Sidon has been suggested to have recreated this fire-breathing effect. A torch may have been inserted through a circular hole that is carved in the

Marble statue of the Mithraic leontocephaline figure from Sidon, 2nd–4th century AD.

back of the head to give the theatrical effect of flames spewing forth from his gaping mouth.[38] Dramatic use of lighting (and its absence) played a key role in creating atmosphere in the Mithraic cave-temples. This is apparent from the frequent depiction of torches in iconography and the discovery of many oil lamps in Mithraea. As a sun god, Mithras himself was a source of illumination, and lions (who were regarded as fiery creatures) were appropriate companions. The name of the Leontocephaline is unknown, though it has been suggested he may be Aion, a god of time.[39]

INITIATION AND RITUAL

The initiated were called *syndexioi* ('united by the handshake').[40] Devotees of Mithraism ascended through seven stages of initiation. Beginning as a Raven (*Corvus*), the member advanced to the level of Bridegroom (*Nymphus*), then Soldier (*Miles*), Lion (*Leo*), Persian (*Perses*), Sun-Runner (*Heliodromos*) and finally Father (*Pater*). Each of these corresponded to one of the seven *planetes* ('wanderers'): Mercury, Venus, Mars, Jupiter, the Moon, the Sun and Saturn.[41] A ladder-like mosaic ran down the middle of the Mithraeum of Felicissimus, Ostia Antica, that depicts each of these grades. At the bottom, a raven accompanied by a beaker and caduceus staff of Hermes/Mercury represents the first degree. The panel for the Bridegroom is damaged, but the surviving lamp and diadem are evocative of Venus. Icons of an army bag, spear and helmet are appropriate for the Soldier. A sistrum, thunderbolt and fire shovel are used for the fiery Lion class. The Persian is represented by the crescent Moon, a hooked sword and a

Mosaic running down the central aisle at the Mithraeum of Felicissimus, Ostia Antica, 2nd–3rd century AD.

scythe. A torch, solar crown and charioteer's whip denotes initiation as a Sun-Runner. The symbols that signified achieving the final stage of Father are a Patera libation bowl, rod, Phrygian cap and sickle. Inscriptions of Mithraic initiates identified as all these different ranks are found throughout

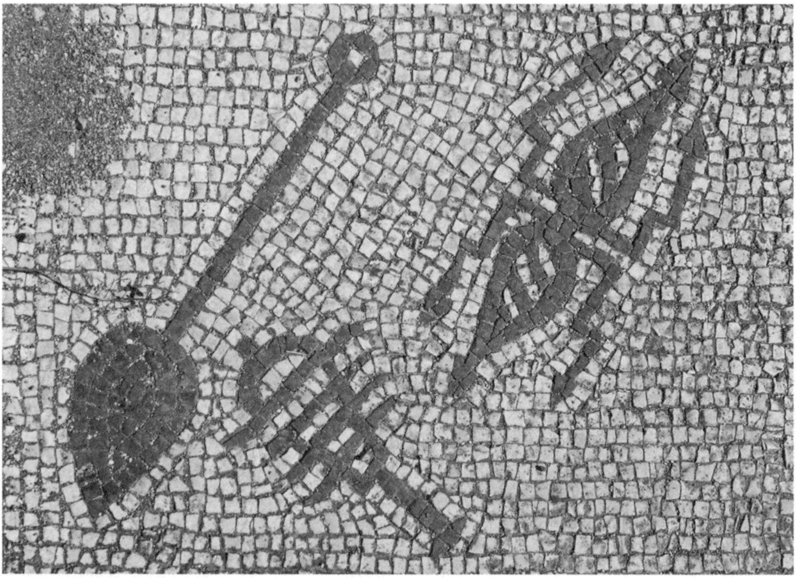

The Lion (Leo).
The Persian (Perses).

The Sun-Runner (Heliodromos).
The Father (Pater).

the empire, though the Lion and Father occur most frequently.[42] Newly initiated Ravens seem to have been assigned menial tasks, serving during meals and cleaning, while higher levels corresponded with more priestly roles.[43] There appears to have been a certain level of flexibility in the adoption of the grade system by different Mithraea, references indicating a reduction of the hierarchy to core levels at temples further away from Rome.[44]

Army men were most predominant in the cult, though there are inscriptions that reference citizens from other professions, including bureaucrats and merchants.[45] The *Invictus* epithet of Mithras was probably very appealing to soldiers in the cult, the god lending some of his invincibility to devotees on the battlefield.[46] Slaves were among the initiated, and no doubt required permission from their masters to join.[47] The opportunity for social advancement probably influenced many people's decision to be initiated, as well as the appeal of being part of a privileged group who shared meals together. Multiple generations from a single family are sometimes listed as initiates, fathers likely encouraging the recruitment of sons.[48] There is no evidence of an initiation or ongoing membership fee, but some sort of payment seems likely for covering costs of rituals, catering and upkeep of a Mithraeum.[49] The loyalty of the initiated to the imperial family is indicated in the many votive inscriptions that either ask Mithras to protect the emperor or are dedicated to the god on his behalf.[50] Textual sources suggest that at least two Roman emperors were among the initiated. Commodus allowed a Mithraeum to be constructed in the imperial palace and was reported to have profaned the symbolic violence of initiation ordeals (see below) with actual murder.[51] The emperor Julian (known as the 'apostate' for his restoration of state paganism) showed devotion to Mithraism. He praised the god in his writings and even personally performed the initiation of a friend named Himerius.[52] Membership seems to have been exclusively male. As evident from the visual material discussed above, there is a lack of female figures in Mithraic iconography and myth. Women do not appear in surviving membership lists and depictions of the initiated. However, in Porphyry's discussion of the various degrees of initiation, he also refers to female participants by the term 'Hyenas'. This is highly unflattering. Hyenas in the Classical world were portrayed as carrion-eating beasts who could produce a strangely human laugh and were believed to be capable of changing sex.[53] This term was probably used in reference to the ideological existence, rather than physical presence, of women in the cult.[54]

Little was written on the process of initiation for the different grades. Porphyry, however, does provide an interesting detail on part of the ritual for becoming a Lion. As the Lion class is associated with fire, it is not appropriate to use water for purification, as the liquid is hostile to flames. Instead, honey is used for washing the initiates' hands and purifying their tongues.[55] Tertullian describes the ritual for becoming a 'soldier of Mithras', but it is unclear whether by this phrase he is referring to the Soldier class or initiation more generally:

> When he is initiated in the cave, in the very camp of darkness, a crown is offered to him at sword-point,

> as if in imitation of martyrdom, and then when the crown has been placed on his head, he is urged to raise his hands and dash it from his head on to his shoulders, if he can, saying that Mithras is his crown.[56]

This account is confirmed visually in a sequence of frescoes from the Mithraeum at Santa Maria Capua Vetere.[57] The naked male initiate is blindfolded with two men conducting the procedure. He initially stumbles along, guided by one of the men. The initiate is then made to kneel with his hands tied behind his back and threatened with a sword before the weapon is thrown down before him. In the next scene, the blindfold has been removed and a crown is placed upon his head. This is followed by a depiction of the kneeling initiate being restrained by one of the men, who is holding him from behind by the shoulders with one foot pressed down upon his calves. In the final scene the initiate lies stretched out prostrate on the ground. The two men stand at either end of his hands and feet. Lying as though dead, he has undergone a symbolic execution and test of courage.[58] Evidence of feigning bodily injury and simulating death in ritual is also apparent from a sword blade found within the Mithraeum of Rigel/Schwarzwald that had been deliberately broken in half and reattached with a hoop in the centre that is large enough to fit around an individual's torso.[59] The use of blindfolds and bindings are noted by the Christian author Ambrosiaster (fourth century AD), who also mentions a curious detail about mimicking animal behaviour for the Raven and Lion grades: 'Their eyes are blindfolded that they may not refuse to be foully abused. Some moreover beat their wings together like a bird, and croak like ravens, and others roar like lions. Yet others are pushed across ditches filled with water, their hands having previously been tied with the intestines of a chicken.'[60] Masks may have been used in the adoption of these animal personas, as is suggested by the depiction of a bird-headed figure encountered in Mithraic feasting imagery.[61] Ambrosiaster also mentions a fifty-day fast, twenty days spent freezing in the snow and two days of ritual floggings.[62]

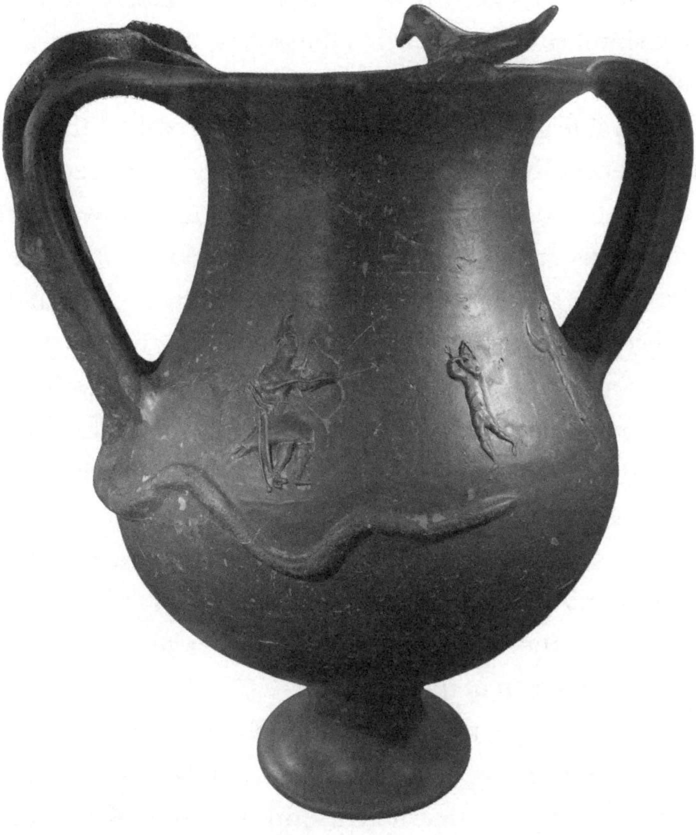

Krater from Mithraeum at Mainz depicting initiation scene, 2nd century AD.

Further visual evidence supports the use of humiliating and distressing scenarios in Mithraic ritual. A terrified initiate is represented on a krater (dated AD 120–40) found beneath the floor of the Mithraeum at Mainz, Germany.[63] He is naked and holds up his hands, which are bound together, to protect his face. For in front of him sits a Mithraic priest, bearded and wearing the Phrygian cap, who holds an arrow poised in a bow aimed at the initiate. Another bearded man stands behind the naked and beardless figure. This mystagogue is making a gesture of declaration, probably explaining the significance of the act to the initiate. Sizing is used to further denote the already apparent power relations, with the vulnerable initiate depicted on a smaller scale to the men administering the initiatory rite. Comparison between this scene and those of Mithras causing a spring to flow from a rock with his arrow has led to the suggestion that this rite functioned as ritual mimesis of the water miracle.[64] Archery thus becomes a purificatory process, enabling waters of life to gush forth from the individual. A Mithraic procession of four people is depicted on the other side of the krater. They are dressed in differing costumes, perhaps representing various levels of initiation. The wearing of a diadem and holding of a whip may identify one of these characters as a Sun-Runner. Additional decoration is found in the moulded snake that slithers up one of the handles and the raven perched on the rim of the vessel.

It is unclear if Mithraism promised afterlife benefits as a reward for surviving its ordeal rituals. The emperor Julian (AD 331–363) reports that he was introduced to the cult by none other than Hermes the Psychopompos, who spoke to him, saying, 'I have granted you the knowledge of your father Mithras. Keep his commandments, and thus secure for yourself a cable and sure anchorage throughout your life, and when you must depart from the world you can with good hopes adopt him as your guardian god.'[65] Further hints are found in a passage from of the pagan author Celsus (second century AD), whose work survives in quotation by Origen.[66] He describes the astrological ascent destined for an initiate. The Mithraic soul passes through seven heavenly gates, each associated with a metal and planet. The first is the lead gate of Saturn, followed by the tin gate of Venus, the bronze gate of Jupiter and the iron gate of Mercury. The gate of Mars is uneven and varied in quality. The highest are the silver gate of the Moon and the golden gate of the Sun. It has been suggested that these were thought to be unlocked by the keys held by the lion-headed figure.[67] Whether this indicates that initiates were provided with understanding on the nature of the afterlife or not, it certainly reflects the importance of astronomical bodies and ascending grades in the cult. There are many thankful ex-voto inscriptions dedicated to Mithras. A certain devotee named Valerianus Petalus called Mithras 'my helper' (*adiutor*), but exactly how he helped his initiated has been lost to time.[68]

One of the most easily accessible places for people who hope to experience the mysteries of Mithras today is the London Mithraeum. Discovered in 1954, the building was moved from its original site. It has since been reconstructed as a subterranean structure beneath the Bloomberg building in Walbrook, London. Coming in from street level, a visitor enters a gallery used for contemporary art installations alongside a display of ancient objects found in excavations of the Roman Mithraeum. Descending below, visitors enter a dark room in which they can walk around the archaeological remains of the temple. The space is brought alive with an immersive and atmospheric ten-minute multisensory experience. Recordings of ancient-inspired music, Latin prayers drawn from inscriptions and chanting echo through the space as a theatrical fog fills the room. Sheets of light fall from the ceiling through the mist. Light and darkness alternate, with a depiction of the tauroctony becoming fully illuminated at the apex of the ceremony. The audio track concludes with a recording of men socializing and feasting, suggestive of the ceremonial meals once shared on the stone benches lining the temple.[69]

The restored Mithraeum beneath the Bloomberg building in Walbrook, London, founded in the 3rd century AD.

Votive standard of the Jupiter Dolichenus cult, 2nd–3rd century AD.

Mithras was not the only 'Eastern' mystery god that was favoured with the Roman army, a related cult being that of Jupiter Dolichenus.[70] The god was perceived as being Syrian, his epithet derived from the city of Doliche (modern Dülük in Turkey's Gaziantep Province). There is considerably less evidence for his cult and it did not enjoy the popularity of Mithraism. The cult developed in the second century AD, enjoying a brief period of prevalence before going into decline in the third century. Its demise resulted from the destruction of multiple sanctuaries, including the Sassanian capture and sacking of Doliche itself. This form of Jupiter is depicted as a bearded man with his usual thunderbolt (and occasionally his eagle), but with additional elements. He is armed in military garb, wielding a double-headed axe as a second weapon and wearing a Phrygian cap. Jupiter Dolichenus is usually portrayed standing on the back of a striding bull, recalling an old theme in Anatolian iconography of depicting storm gods atop the virile animal.[71] His consort is Juno Dolichena, who parallels her husband in her stance on the back of a deer. The pair appear together in relief on triangular votive metal plaques distinct to the cult, often accompanied by other divine personas – winged Victory, the Sun and Moon, the twin brothers Castor and Pollux. Around twenty temples to Jupiter Dolichenus are known, though there is little textual documentation that attests to the rituals conducted within them.

FIVE

THE SAMOTHRACIAN MYSTERIES AND THE KABEIROI

The island of Samothrace in the northeast Aegean was renowned in the ancient Greek world for its mystery religion. Though not as well known today, it was the second most popular mystery cult in antiquity after the rites of Eleusis.[1] Our earliest evidence of religious practice dates from the seventh century BC, with veneration of the cult continuing after the Roman domination of Greece. Most of the surviving archaeological remains date to the Hellenistic period, with patronage offered by the Macedonian kings. Plutarch reports that it was during initiation at Samothrace that the parents of Alexander the Great had apparently met, his mother Olympias being noted for her interest in exotic religious experiences.[2] At the Sanctuary of the Great Gods on Samothrace, the focal point of veneration was a group of chthonic deities. Herodotus identifies them as an assembly of gods known collectively as the Kabeiroi (or Cabeiri).[3] He had visited Samothrace and was likely initiated into the mystery cult. Herodotus reports that the practice of crafting boundary markers in the likeness of Hermes was adopted by the Athenians from Samothrace. A herm took the form of a squared pillar of marble, topped with a male bust and a

Marble herm from Siphnos, 6th century BC.

phallus prominently carved on its front. The sacred story about their origin was apparently revealed during the Samothracian mysteries.[4] In addition to being accused of profaning the Eleusinian Mysteries, Alcibiades was also blamed for the mutilation of Athens' *hermai* that occurred during the Peloponnesian War.[5] The impious vandalism was seen as a bad omen for the city.

Mysteries associated with the Kabeiroi were also conducted at a temple on Lemnos and at Thebes in Boeotia. The individual identities of the Kabeiroi are somewhat obscured by the secrecy required of initiates. Pausanias thus writes, 'I must ask the curious to forgive me if I keep silence as to who the Kabeiroi are, and what is the nature of the ritual performed in honour of them.'[6] While several Classical authors do identify the names and number of gods revered at Samothrace, there is no agreement among them. Mnaseas of Patara (*c.* 200 BC) gives them as Axieros, Axiokersa, Axiokersos and Kadmilos, figures who have been identified as Demeter, Persephone, Hades and Hermes.[7] Other sources suggest that the Kabeiroi is another name for the Dioscuri, the twin brothers Castor and Pollux who make up the constellation Gemini.[8]

However, there is even dispute about the use of the term 'Kabeiroi' for the collective group. Inscriptions found at Samothrace generally use the designation of *Theoi Megaloi* ('Great Gods') to refer to them.[9] The historian Hugh Bowden proposes that the evidence on the nature of the gods worshipped at Samothrace is confusing and contradictory because they were nameless shadowy figures, that 'nobody knew very much about . . . gods who could not be identified and about whom stories could not be told. These are effectively gods without myths.'[10] Individuals may have interpreted the experience (which may not have been clearly explained to them) differently. Since these figures were not assigned a concrete identity, understanding of who they were would be susceptible to change over time. Mythology of the Latin period claimed that the Penates, gods of the household, came from Samothrace.[11] They were brought to Rome by Aeneas via Troy. Whether this affected the experience of the Mysteries for a Roman citizen is hard to say.

BEING AN INITIATE AT SAMOTHRACE

The rites were conducted at night-time. They seem to have promised both cosmological knowledge and protection from the Great Gods. Diodorus Siculus provides clues on some of the appealing rewards bestowed on those inducted in the Mysteries:

> Now the details of the initiatory rite are guarded among the matters not to be divulged and are communicated to the initiates alone; but the fame has travelled wide of how these gods appear to mankind and bring unexpected aid to those initiates of theirs who call upon them in the midst of perils. The claim is also made that men who have taken part in the mysteries become both more pious and more just and better in every respect than they were before.[12]

It seems that theophany and morality were on offer to the faithful at Samothrace.

It is at this sanctuary that the famed Winged Victory of Samothrace was found, a Hellenistic sculpture of Nike discovered during archaeological excavations of the site in 1863. Now in the Louvre, it depicts the windswept goddess alighting the bow of a ship. It was likely dedicated to the Great Gods (whoever they were) following a naval victory, for this cult was particularly popular with sailors who, among other membership benefits, were promised protection from perils faced at sea.[13] Votives of seashells and fish

Winged Victory of Samothrace, 3rd–2nd century BC.

hooks offered by grateful seamen of more modest means have also been found at the site, which was located on a maritime crossroads. Shipwrecks were far too common and much-feared in the ancient imagination for voyagers to not seek divine aid. After surveying many votive offerings that had been left by appreciative sailors at Samothrace, Diagoras of Melos is said to have cynically remarked, 'There would be many more of these if those who were not saved had made declarations.'[14]

There were no requirements of age, gender, status or nationality. An initiate could be Greek or non-Greek, slave or free.[15] Still, initiates tended to be male. The first stage of initiation was known as the *muesis*, with a second degree called the *epopteia*.[16] Though a major festival was held at the sanctuary in midsummer, one could be initiated at any time. It was possible to attain both levels of investiture on the same day. Contrasting with the annual experience offered at Eleusis, this is probably a reflection of the challenges posed by getting to the island.[17] Tacitus reports that Germanicus attempted journeying to Samothrace in the first century AD, but was prevented by unfavourable winds.[18]

Varro and Hippolytus reported that two bronze ithyphallic male statues (which may have had a connection to the sacred story alluded to by Herodotus) once flanked the doorway of the building in which the secret rituals were performed.[19] While an inscription of the Roman period found within the sanctuary warns that 'Non-initiates may not enter the sacred building,'[20] the exact structure where the Mysteries were conducted is unclear. There are several possibilities. Scholars long believed that this occurred inside a rectangular building known as the Anaktoron.[21] Benches ran along two of its walls, which would allow for viewing of the spectacle. Another building, which has been dubbed the Hieron, has also been proposed.[22] It was likewise rectangular and lined with benches. A lustral basin was at the entrance, with a hearth in the centre of the room. A raised apse was at the far end, a focal point perhaps, on which an image could be displayed. The tholos temple known as the Arsinoeion is another contender, the largest enclosed round building in the Greek world.[23] It is named after Arsinoe II (316–270 BC), an inscription above its door identifying the building as being dedicated by the Ptolemaic queen. Notable are its altars and relief panels that surrounded the interior walls, which feature alternating bucrania (imagery of sacrificial ox skulls) and rosettes.

The most likely candidate, however, is the Hall of the Choral Dancers, which is the largest building within the complex and at the centre of the site.[24] It is named for its Hellenistic frieze that surrounded the building, sculpted with about nine hundred maidens who hold hands, dance and play musical instruments. Partaking in or viewing such ecstatic movements performed by religious personnel was likely part of initiation. One interpretation of the frieze is that it depicts celebratory dancing that accompanied the mythological wedding of Harmonia and Cadmus.[25] The myth reports these nuptials occurred after Harmonia was abducted by Cadmus from her island home of Samothrace. She is most known for the necklace that she received on her wedding day. The cursed jewellery brought madness and misfortune to successive generations of heroes who inherited it. The Necklace of

Harmonia was famously used by Polynice to bribe Eriphyle. Seduced by the pretty trinket, she convinced her husband to join an ill-fated war on Thebes that led to his death. Harmonia's brother Iasion was regarded as the founder of the Samothracian Mysteries. Like the search of Demeter at Eleusis, part of initiation seems to have involved a search for Harmonia.[26] There is evidence of sacrifices, the pouring of libations and the sharing of a communal meal, but much like the Great Gods themselves, the rest of the mystic experience is shadowy.

At the conclusion of the initiation, participants were presented with a purple fillet that was tied around the waist as a protective talisman.[27] Literary sources report that magnetic iron rings were also tokens of initiation.[28] Several have been found at the site, likely valued for the seemingly magical ability of magnetized iron. Before leaving the sanctuary with these souvenirs of their experience, many happy participants left inscriptions as a record of their initiation. An Athenian man named Isidorus of the first or second century BC reports on marble that 'as an initiate, great-hearted, he saw the sacred light of the two Kabeiroi in Samothrace and the pure rites of Demeter in Eleusis.'[29] The name given here to the Samothracian gods is interesting, but we are still no closer to identifying the Great Gods. Of the sacred light that illuminated these figures for people like Isidorus, only the ceramic oil lamps used in their rites remain.

SIX

ORPHISM AND THE DIONYSIAN MYSTERIES

Two connected mystery religions were the cult of Dionysus and its later derivative Orphism. Examination of the soul features in both, with recurring imagery of dismemberments and restorations. The Greek fertility god Dionysus, also known as Bacchus (the latter name being adopted by the Romans for the god they called Liber), was associated with the creation and consumption of wine. He was perceived as a latecomer to the Olympian pantheon who had come from the east. In addition to the term *mystes*, those initiated into his rites were often referred to as *bacchoi*.[1] An Athenian named Icarius was credited with having received knowledge of viticulture from the god and shared this gift with humankind. At first this was not received well. The shepherds who first tasted the beverage were convinced in their drunken state that they had been poisoned and subsequently killed Icarius.[2] In addition to his intoxicating character, Dionysus was the patron of drama. He was also believed to hold sway over fearsome and exotic wild animals, and is often represented as bringing his rites to new territory upon the back of a panther. Wherever Dionysus goes, wine springs up from the earth, or whole bodies of water are transformed into alcoholic drink. The god's followers were a posse of women called maenads and the horny hybrid goat-men known as satyrs. In art and myth, they drink, dance and produce orgiastic music for the god, dressed in animal skins. Some gyrate while holding snakes in their hands. Others engage in unrestrained sexual activity. Associated with his worship was the wielding of a protective staff known as a *thyrsus*, held by these followers or the god himself. It consisted of a stalk of giant fennel that was twisted with ivy vines and topped with a pine cone. Plato critiques that 'they say in the mysteries "the thyrsus-bearers are many, but the mystics few".'[3] Perhaps not all who were caught up in the ecstatic rites of the gods understood their full significance.

Theatres were dedicated to Dionysus and the performance of plays at public festivals was part of his worship,

Tondo of a red-figure Attic cup depicting a satyr playing the aulos before Dionysus, 490–480 BC. The god holds the thyrsus in one hand and a grapevine in the other.

Two actors are about to put on satyr masks. A third actor has donned his mask. He gleefully thrusts his pelvis forward, having taken on the persona of his character under the influence of Dionysus. They all wear leather shorts to which are attached a phallus and tail. Apulian red-figure bell krater, *c.* 410–380 BC.

most notably at the City Dionysia in Athens. In addition to the violence that was the subject of many of the plays, actual bloody sacrifice was enacted as part of the spectacle at his altar on stage.[4] Masks, with their theatrical notions of disguising and taking on alternative identities, were symbolic of the god. The mask was also a highly portable image that could be used for cultic purposes. Vase paintings depict a venerated figure of Dionysus, consisting of a tree or pillar made anthropomorphic by the attachment of a mask.[5] Hugh Bowden elaborates on their figurative role:

Detail of an Apulian red-figure calyx-krater depicting a follower of Dionysus (who wields a thyrsus) receiving a theatrical mask from the seated god, *c.* 380 BC. A drunk satyr is perched on an amphora behind.

> The mask could be thought of in the same way as a cult statue, or perhaps as the hiera carried in the procession of the Eleusinian Mysteries: a sacred representation of the god . . . Bacchic rites give bacchants the opportunity to see the god without his mask . . . a trance state in which they might meet Dionysus unmasked.[6]

Visual evidence suggests that dressing up in mythical roles may have played a key role in cult ritual. Dionysus could be portrayed as effeminate, as could his male devotees. It was men wearing masks who played the female roles in Greek dramas performed in his honour. The god was given the epithet Eleutherios ('the liberator'), and the wearing of masks and drinking of wine offered freedom from social restraints.[7]

A key feature of the Bacchic Mysteries were nocturnal rituals in which dancing played a central role. This began within the city, with a public sacrifice and a procession open to all. Initiates were then led from the civilized realm, going beyond the safety of their city walls into the untamed natural world for wild activities in surrounding wooded hills and caves.[8] This inverted world of the mountainside hosted the secret aspects of the cult. A mystic wine-drinking ritual was likely involved, in contrast with more controlled *symposia* (the social institution of drinking parties held by aristocratic men of the city). During these frenzied rites, an individual might lose cognizance of where they were or what they were doing. In *ekstasis,* the rapturous and disorientating state of ecstasy, a Dionysian devotee was said to stand outside themselves. The condition of *enthousiasmos* followed, in which the person's body was filled with the god.[9] Though direct contact with the divine was desired, it had the potential to be dangerous. In the account of Dionysus' own birth, his mortal mother Semele is fried to a crisp when she sees her lover Zeus in his thunderous true form.[10] The king of the gods retrieves the pre-term baby from the charred remains and has his son sewn into his own thigh. Baby Dionysus is able to finish developing there, and is subsequently born from his father's leg. Dionysus was thus given the epithet *Dimetor* ('twice-born').[11]

Resistance to divine experience could be even worse than the awesome terror of direct contact. In the myth of Pentheus, the king of Thebes denies that Dionysus is a god. Pentheus both refuses to partake in and bans the ecstatic cult of the wine god from entering his city. Dionysus responds by inciting all the women of Thebes into an ecstatic frenzy. They abandon their homes, dancing and parading wildly in the mountainside. Pentheus has Dionysus imprisoned, but he escapes easily. The chains binding him simply fall off and the penitentiary doors open at his divine command. The wine god disguises himself and convinces Pentheus to spy on what mischief the women are up to in the forest. The king cross-dresses in female clothes to aid his investigation, for Dionysus is a god of inversion and the destruction of traditional boundaries. Although Pentheus hides in a tree, he is quickly spotted by the women. In a state of divine madness, they mistake Pentheus for a wild animal. Pulling him down from the tree, they violently kill the king, tearing him apart with their bare hands. In Dionysian myth, sacrifice to the god is enacted via the ritual of *sparagmos*, in which a living animal is torn limb from limb. This is usually followed by *omophagia*, the eating of raw animal flesh.[12] It is unclear whether these two rites were actually performed by historical followers of Dionysus or confined to the god's myths. While consumption of raw meat is unlikely, there is one enigmatic inscription from Miletus forbidding anyone 'to throw in the omophagion [meat eaten raw]' prior to the priestess of Dionysus having done so first.[13] Blood and wine are used to evoke each other in Dionysian myths and ritual.

The story of Pentheus is most famously depicted by Euripides (fifth century BC) in *The Bacchae*. This tragedy itself was one of the plays entered in the drama competition held in honour of the god at the City Dionysia. A chorus of initiated Bacchae, who lend their name to the text, sing 'Blessed is he who, being fortunate and knowing the rites of the gods, keeps his life pure and has his soul initiated into the Bacchic revels, dancing in inspired frenzy over the mountains with

Pentheus is about to be ripped limb from limb by two Theban women on this Apulian red-figure oinochoe, 375–350 BC.

holy purifications . . . who brandishing the thyrsus, garlanded with ivy, serves Dionysus.'[14] At one point in the play the hubristic king asks about the nature of these Dionysian Mysteries, to which the (disguised) god responds, 'They cannot be told to mortals uninitiated in Bacchic revelry . . . It is not lawful for you to hear, but they are worth knowing.'[15] The drama concludes with Pentheus' own mother Agave, who took part in her son's murder, carrying his (mask-like) dismembered head on a stick back to Thebes. In a moment of great pathos, she returns to her senses and only then realizes the horror of what she has done.

After spreading his rites, Dionysus descended to the Underworld in order to bring back his mother Semele. The salvation Dionysus provides to his mother bestows upon her a new status. She is transformed into a goddess (who presides over frenzy) and given the new name Thyone.[16] Just as wine is created out of crushed grapes, so too Semele is destroyed in order to be elevated.[17] Following his journey below, Dionysus ascends to the heavens to take his place among the gods as a new Olympian. Dionysus is thus a liminal figure, his intoxicating mysteries providing truth on the extremes he experienced of life and death. This is apparent in small bone initiation tokens found at Pontic Olbia of the fifth century BC. They have various inscriptions including examples that name Dionysus and juxtaposing words such as 'life death life' or 'truth falsehood'.[18]

Certain truths were to be found in the *liknon*, a winnowing basket in which sacred objects of the gods were carried in processions.[19] Likely symbols that were revealed to the initiated include a sacred winecup, mask, mirror, grapes, a phallus and perhaps even live serpents that were apparently waved about in Dionysian worship. The *Apologia* of Apuleius suggests that some sacred symbols of the god may have been distributed and kept by initiates, and venerated privately in their homes:

> I have been initiated into various of the Greek mysteries, and preserve with the utmost care certain emblems and mementoes of my initiation with which the priests presented me. There is nothing abnormal or unheard of in this. Those of you here present who have been initiated into the mysteries of father Liber [Dionysus] alone, know what you keep hidden at home, safe from all profane touch and the object of your silent veneration.[20]

This text is a defence that the writer presented before a proconsul in Sabratha in AD 158–9 on being accused of witchcraft. Driven by his keen pursuit of knowledge, Apuleius (same author of *The Golden Ass*, which provided us with much information on the cult of Isis) was initiated into many different mystery religions.

While both genders partook in Dionysian rites, the more frenzied aspects of his cult are particularly associated with women.[21] A group of female worshippers from Delphi were known for their night-time dances on the slopes of Mt Parnassus in adoration of the wine god. On one occasion, they became so caught up in ecstasy that the disorientated women ended up in the marketplace of the nearby city of Amphissa.[22] There they collapsed in exhaustion. At this time

Dancing maenad lost in a Dionysian state of ecstasy.
Paestan red-figure skyphos, *c.* 340–320 BC.

Delphi and Amphissa were on opposite sides of a war feud. The women of Amphissa therefore formed a guard around their Delphic counterparts to protect them from the men of the city. Once they had arisen from slumber, the Amphissian women gave them food and escorted these Dionysian devotees back to Delphi. Pausanias reports that the temple of Dionysus at Bryseae in the Peloponnese contained a statue of the god that could only be viewed by female worshippers.[23] In this particular manifestation of his cult, women alone were allowed to partake in the sacred Mysteries of Dionysus.

RAUCOUS ROMANS

In the Roman world, elements of the Dionysian Mysteries found continuity in the Bacchanalia. They arrived in Rome at the end of the third century BC, via Etruria and Greek colonies in southern Italy.[24] Reports of its entrance into Rome claim that initially it was exclusively for women. This changed when a Campanian woman named Paculla Annia began to initiate men.[25] The unofficial, secretive and privately funded nature of bacchanals during the Republic made them prone to suspicion and scandal. The most famous account, by the Roman historian Livy (59 BC–AD 17), portrays the rites as loud, debauched and encouraging criminal behaviour:

> There were initiatory rites which at first were imparted to a few . . . To the religious element in them were added the delights of wine and feasts, that the minds of a larger number might be attracted. When wine had inflamed their minds all varieties of corruption first began to be practiced, since each one had at hand the chance of gratifying the particular desire to which he was naturally inclined. There was promiscuous mating of free men and women. The cult was also a source for the supply of false witnesses, forged documents and wills, and perjured evidence. Likewise, were the poisonings and secret murders, so that at times not even the bodies were found for burial . . . This violence was concealed, because amid the howling and the crash of drums and cymbals no cry

> of the sufferers could be heard as the debauchery and murders proceeded.[26]

With hair dishevelled, the Bacchae wildly gyrated their bodies into distorted positions and blabbered prophecies. Taking their flaming torches down to the Tiber, they plunged them into the river and brought them out still burning (they were apparently composed from sulphur and lime). Those who refused to join in were taken to a cave for punishment, bound to some kind of machine and otherwise reported to have been spirited away by the gods. Murders and torture mentioned in the text are likely a distortion of cult practice that involved the infliction of a symbolic death upon an initiate.

Livy's wild narrative should be treated with caution, although it does reflect actual suppression of the cult that was decreed by the state. Such secret meetings, especially those that allowed for the mixing of men and women, were feared for their potential to arouse plots against Rome. A notable edict of 186 BC, the *Senatus consultum de Bacchanalibus*, was circulated in response to the bacchanalia.[27] A copy of the text survives on a bronze tablet found in Calabria that prohibited Romans from participation in bacchanals. Exemption in certain special cases required approval by the Senate. While not banning the cult completely, the document shows an attempt to control its size, organization and priesthoods.[28] It functioned as a display of the (collective) authority of the Senate over (individual) citizens.

DIONYSIAN DEPICTIONS

Visually, our best source on the cult in the Roman world is the so-called Villa of Mysteries on the outskirts of Pompeii. It is named for its famous fresco of 70–60 BC that decorates Room 5, this apartment within the house bearing the form of a *triclinium* (dining room).[29] Against a striking red background are depicted what appear to be scenes of initiation into the Mysteries of Dionysus.[30] Female figures dominate ritual scenes that surround the walls of the room. Dionysus is portrayed in the centre, reclining on the lap of a woman who is identified as either his mother Semele or wife Ariadne. On their left is a group of satyrs, one of which stands behinds and holds up a mask, while another spies the reflection of this theatrical object being mirrored back at him within a bowl. To the right, a woman is lifting a veil that conceals some secret object (resembling a phallus) within a *liknon* basket.

Most evocative of the humiliations and intimidation experienced when undergoing initiation is the image of a downcast kneeling woman, her robe stripped to the hip and her head cradled in the lap of another. She is being flagellated by a winged female figure who holds the raised whip in one hand and makes a gesture of aversion towards the unveiled *liknon*. There are several candidates for the identification of this allegorical figure, but the most convincing theory is that she personifies Ignorance. Through initiation the individual overcomes the agonizing state of initial ignorance, transitioning to a position of knowledge.[31] *Phasmata* (apparitions) are mentioned in relation to the Dionysian

A satyr holds a wine cup before a man who spies the reflection of a theatrical mask held behind him by another man. Fresco from the Villa of Mysteries, 70–60 BC.

A woman lifts a veil off a concealed object. The winged allegorical figure on the right raises a whip to flagellate a woman in the next image. Fresco from the Villa of Mysteries, 70–60 BC.

Mysteries, and it is possible that the illustration depicts such an experience.[32]

Next to the flogged initiate is a woman who dances naked and clashes a small pair of cymbals above her head. Behind her a fully robed woman wields a thyrsus. Other figures attending the ceremony include a small child reading a text from a scroll (possibly the *hieros logos*, sacred words of instruction for an initiate)[33] and a woman holding a plate of offerings, as well as satyr musicians playing the lyre and panpipes. One woman flees in terror with a windswept shawl billowing behind her, having witnessed the action taking place in the central scenes.

The initiate being flagellated rests her head on the lap of a seated woman. Another woman dances naked with a pair of cymbals, a robed woman standing behind her holding a thyrsus. Fresco from the Villa of Mysteries, 70–60 BC.

An alternative interpretation associates the iconography of the fresco with prenuptial preparations and allegories of marriage.[34] A purification scene illustrating a woman having lustral water poured before her by attendants, and the depiction of the maiden having her hair dressed while looking into a mirror held by a cupid, speak to this point. The imagery may be designed to evoke both, drawing an allegorical connection between initiation into the Mysteries and the transitional state of being a bride.

A wealth of Dionysian imagery is also found in the recurring theme of multiple Roman marble funerary sarcophagi. These depict triumphant processions in which the god is accompanied by maenads and satyrs who ride animals, dance, make music and drink wine. Grape vines entwine their way through the scenes. While this is not a scene of initiation, the imagery is suggestive of the well-being expected by the dead who had knowledge of the Mysteries.[35] Though not every classical artwork depicting Dionysian revelries was produced in the context of the Mysteries, it is likely that those that had undergone initiation viewed these images differently to the non-initiated.[36]

Scenes of Dionysian revelry on the marble sarcophagus of Maconiana Severiana, a young woman from a senatorial family, AD 210–220.

Visual representation of Dionysus is frequent on ceramics that were buried alongside the dead as grave goods, some depictions explicitly associating him with the afterlife. An Apulian volute krater (wine mixing bowl), currently housed at Ohio's Toledo Museum of Art, depicts Dionysus visiting the Underworld. Dating from 335–325 BC, the mythological figures depicted are labelled with their names in Greek.[37] Dionysus approaches the palace of Hades and Persephone in the central scene. The king of the Underworld sits enthroned, holding a sceptre topped with a bird, with his wife standing next to him. The queen wields a cross-torch that evokes her nocturnal Eleusinian rites. The god of wine clasps hands with Hades. This may be interpreted as a gesture of arrival, departure or negotiation in which Dionysus secures his initiated *bacchoi* a better afterlife allotment.[38] Surrounding figures in the Underworld include maenads, a satyr, the wing-footed Hermes Psychopompos, Pentheus and his mother/murderer Agave. Tied to a leash below the palace sits Hades' dog Cerberus, who guards the gates of the Underworld to prevent the dead from escaping. In a charming passage from Horace's Ode to Bacchus, the usually ferocious three-headed beast gently fawns on Dionysus during his Underworld adventure: 'You were graced with golden [drinking] horn when Cerberus saw you: he was harmless, and softly wagged his tail. As you were leaving, he licked your legs and feet with all three of his tongues.'[39] While Dionysus is not ruler of the Underworld, he has power there and in his presence the kingdom of the dead is changed. On the reverse of the Toledo vase a nude youth stands within a tomb shrine, this presumably being an idealized representation of the deceased individual with whom this vessel was buried.

Dionysus was similarly evoked in funerary inscriptions. An epitaph from Bulgaria compares a deceased woman to Semele, the analogy to his mother reflecting the hope of being rescued from death by the god. The inscription invokes Dionysus with the epithet *lusiponos* ('releaser from pain').[40] Another example from Philippi describes a dead boy as a satyr who is welcomed into a bucolic meadow in the afterlife by female initiates.[41] A *mystes* from Macedonia is said to have broken free from the binding vines of Hades.[42] An inscription from Cumae indicates that an exclusive area was designated in which only Dionysian initiates could be buried, presumably reflecting a group expectation of a different allotment in the afterlife.[43] This salvific association of Dionysus was expanded on in the mystery religion that has become known as Orphism, to which we will now turn.

ORPHEUS AND THE GOLDEN TABLETS

Orphism was based around rituals ascribed to the mythical hero Orpheus, with Dionysus remaining a central figure. Underworld vases are known that depict a very similar scene to the Toledo example discussed above, but the figure who approaches Hades' palace is Orpheus.[44] Since the legendary musician descended to the land of the dead and returned (although he was unsuccessful in his attempt to retrieve his deceased wife), he too could guide the initiated through the Underworld. This ancient religion of Orphism is not to be confused with the twentieth-century artistic school of the same name, an offshoot of Cubism founded by Robert and Sonia Delaunay.[45] Orpheus was an artist extraordinaire whose magical singing and playing of the lyre charmed gods, humans, animals and even trees and rocks.[46] After his death, ripped apart by the frenzied maenads of Dionysus, his head was reported to have continued singing.[47] Orpheus was reputed to have authored mystery texts, the content of which was relayed to inductees by itinerant priests known as *Orpheotelestai* ('Orphic initiators').[48] The power of the written word and books was central to revelation.

In the myth central to Orphism, Dionysus is given an additional (third!) birth.[49] This version has Persephone as

Orpheus plays his kithara before Persephone and Hades in their underworld palace. Hekate lights the way with two torches. Detail from Apulian red-figure volute krater, 350–325 BC.

his mother. Zeus transforms himself into a snake and rapes the goddess in serpentine form. The infant Dionysus is born from the encounter and destined to be Zeus' successor. This, however, does not sit well with his ever-jealous wife, Hera, who incites the group of primordial gods known as the Titans to kill the child. Luring baby Dionysus in with toys (which include a shining mirror), the Titans chop the tiny godling into pieces. Cooking the divine meat over a fire, they then begin to eat the child. As the Titans enjoy their cannibal feast, Athena intervenes and manages to retrieve Dionysus' heart, from which he will be reborn as the son of Zeus and Semele. The king of the gods punishes the Titans, destroying them with his thunderbolts. From the ashes that remain of the Titans (including partially digested bits of Dionysus), humankind is born. Key to all this was the Orphic concept of *soma sema* (σωμα σημα), the idea that the body was a tomb from which the soul should seek to escape.[50] Our bodies have an evil Titanic nature, within which a spark of Dionysian divinity is contained. Initiates sought freedom from a cycle of reincarnation, after which they were granted access to a blissful existence in an exclusive afterlife.[51] Dionysus' closeness to humankind is reflected in that he has experienced something very human that other gods cannot relate to: he is actually killed. Orphics embraced an ascetic lifestyle to maintain spiritual purity. They avoided meat and, more peculiarly, fava (broad) beans. This stems from a belief (adopted from teachings of the philosopher Pythagoras – see below) that the flesh-like *Vicia faba* could contain souls of the dead.[52]

A collection of some 87 'Orphic' Hymns (thought to date from the second or third centuries AD) attributed to Orpheus

Orphic gold tablet inscribed with Greek verse, 4th century BC.

praise various gods, many of whom are the divine patrons of the Mystery religions discussed in this book – the gods of Samothrace, Demeter of Eleusis, Persephone, Cybele, Dionysus and Sabazios. An example hymn to Semele describes a mystic ritual involving a performance of her painful labour: 'They reenact the travail for your son Bacchos, The sacred ritual of the table, and the holy mysteries. Now you, goddess, do I beseech, great Cadmean queen, Always to be gentle-minded towards the initiates.'[53] The hymn to Mnemosyne illustrates her role as the goddess who makes those inducted in the Mysteries remember the secret knowledge they have acquired. She can 'excite the initiates with the memory of the pious ritual and send oblivion away from them'.[54] Mnemosyne is a goddess who makes the initiate remember what to do and say. As patron of Memory, she had a particularly important role in some mnemonic devices that survive in archaeology. These are part of another

Fayum mummy portrait of a boy wearing a necklace capsule, 2nd century AD. It resembles a known pendant case from Petelia that contained a rolled-up Orphic tablet.

group of texts associated with Orphism, which have been inscribed on small sheets of gold and buried with deceased initiates. Around forty examples have been found in Greece and Italy from the fifth century BC right up until the second century AD.[55] Some are in the shape of an ivy leaf, evocative of a strand plucked from a shining Dionysian wreath.[56] Other known examples were rolled, placed within a cylindrical capsule and worn as a pendant, adorning the body as a protective amulet.[57] A Roman mummy portrait from Egypt appears to be wearing one example. Others were placed folded in the mouth (to be spoken), or in the hand (as identification to be presented) of the deceased.[58] The materiality of the tablets (small and not necessarily indicative of wealth) likely added to the mystical value of the inscribed text, gold having strong associations with divinity.

These Orphic gold tablets are occasionally referred to by the German term *totenpass*, passports for the dead.[59] For they were golden tickets that offered instructions on how to navigate the land of the hereafter – advising on the hazards to avoid in the Underworld and containing formulaic responses that a wandering soul should articulate to beings met there. Several warn the dead not to drink from the waters of the river Lethe ('Forgetfulness') but instead to quench their thirst from the pool sacred to Mnemosyne ('Memory').[60] The implication here is that unlike the masses, they will not forget their previous life and will be able to progress to a better part of the Underworld – perhaps Elysium, the exclusive heavenly abode for the heroes of legend. Uninitiated souls who drink from Lethe are reincarnated.[61] The image of dehydrated souls in search of water – or, as described in the *Odyssey*, the blood of a sacrificed sheep around which they swarm, desperate to drink – is familiar in Classical literature.[62]

Texts on the different gold tablets appear to be derived from a common source, utilizing repeated phrases and imagery (though with slight variations).[63] To guards encountered, the individual should declare themselves under the protection of the Queen of the Underworld as a 'son of earth and starry heaven'.[64] In this statement the individual indicates their knowledge of the dual Titanic–Dionysian nature of humanity. Dionysus is evoked in further statements that 'the Bacchic One has released you' and that the initiate has 'Wine as your fortunate honour'.[65] Death is not a source of fear in one text that proclaims, 'Now you have died and now, thrice happy one, you have been born, on this very day.'[66] Several gold tablets have references to atonement and purification undertaken by the soul for unjust deeds. Even apotheosis seems to be on offer: 'Rejoicing enduring what is to be endured! This you have never before experienced. You have become a god instead of a man. You have fallen as a kid into milk. Hail, hail, as you travel on the right, through the Holy Meadow and Groves of Persephone.'[67] The image of the juvenile goat is an enigmatic one, perhaps preserving a fragment of some lost ritual – be it a peculiar form of sacrifice cooked in milk or the bathing in milk of an initiate. Other examples of gold tablets are much shorter and simply identify the dead as members of the initiated with the word *mystes*, occasionally including a salutation to the king and/or queen of the Underworld: 'Posidippus, a pious mystes greets Persephone.'[68] Were the tablets owned and used by the deceased in initiation, abbreviations of a ritual that functioned as a rehearsal of what to do and say in the Underworld? Or were they acquired post-mortem specifically for burial? Hugh Bowden suggests that perhaps 'the gold tablets, in some cases at least, might belong to those who *had not* been initiated, but had instead bought a gold "ticket to heaven" as an alternative way in.'[69] Though they may not have experienced the Mysteries in life, the amuletic tablets would allow them to join a privileged group in death.

Texts buried with the dead could also be written on more perishable materials, apparent from the discovery of the Derveni Papyrus within the remains of a cremation burial near Thessaloniki. Dating from the fourth century BC, it is the only papyrus to survive from ancient Greece and is the oldest surviving manuscript in Europe.[70] Charred and in fragments (the order of which has been variously reconstructed), the document survived the usually unfavourable Greek climate by chance, as it was carbonized from the funeral pyre. Likely a prized possession of the nobleman cremated with it, the papyrus begins with a statement that the text is intended for initiated eyes only: 'I shall sing to those who understand. Close the doors, ye profane ones.'[71] It is largely occupied with a commentary on a poem ascribed to Orpheus that gives a theogony describing the birth of the gods and the ascendency of Zeus. Elements of a mystery ritual are also preserved:

> Magoi perform the sacrifice, as though they were paying an expiatory retribution. Milk and water, with which libations are also made, are poured over the offerings. Countless and many-humped are the cakes

> burnt as offerings, because the souls too are countless. Initiates make a first sacrifice to the Eumenides in the same way as magoi do; for the Eumenides are souls.[72]

The initiates here utilize the expertise of ritual practitioners versed in magic, called *magoi*. They assist in appeasing underworld daimons identified as the Eumenides (another name for Erinyes, the retributive Furies of Greek myth).

The Derveni Papyrus also includes a quotation from the philosopher Heraclitus (*c.* 500 BC).[73] With their interest in the soul and the nature of things, other philosophers were associated with mysteries, blending religion and science in their teachings. Empedocles (fifth century BC) apparently shared knowledge with his followers on how to control the winds and raise the dead, as well as prevent disease and ageing.[74] The most notable of all was Pythagoras (sixth century BC), whose teachings and beliefs formed the basis of Pythagoreanism. Famed for much more than his mathematical theorem that is the chagrin of many a high-school student, sayings attributed to Pythagoras prescribed certain dietary, dress, behavioural and burial requirements.[75] Among these were stipulations to always put your right shoe on first and to spit upon hair/nail trimmings that are cut off in grooming sessions. One should not wear images of the gods on rings, to avoid defiling them.[76] Numbers were regarded with particular significance in the make-up of the universe, with Aristotle (fourth century BC) reporting that 'the so-called Pythagoreans, who were the first to take up mathematics, not only advanced this study, but also having been brought up in it they thought its principles were the principles of all things.'[77] Though he

No beans for me, please! Pythagoras spurns *Vicia faba* in a 16th-century French manuscript illustration.

wrote nothing in his own name, Pythagoras was credited with having authored poems in the guise of Orpheus.[78] His ideas survive in fragments of works penned by his followers. They believed in the transmigration of the soul, that after death an individual was reborn in another human body or as an animal. Pythagoras thus became associated with a vegetarian lifestyle.[79] Pythagorean ideas would influence the cults of Dionysus and Orpheus. Herodotus states that a taboo against burying the dead in woollen clothing, which is often called Orphic or Bacchic, actually had an Egyptian and Pythagorean origin.[80] Over time, legendary claims were made about Pythagoras – that he had taken a return trip to underworld, that he had a golden thigh and that a river had once spoken to him.[81] When bitten by a venomous snake, he apparently killed the deadly creature by biting it back.[82] Pythagorean communities were most prevalent in the Greek cities of Southern Italy.

TROPHONIUS

An interesting parallel to Orphic–Bacchic Mysteries is the oracular cult of Trophonius. Its founding legend held that Trophonius and his brother Agamedes were architects commissioned to build a treasury for King Hyrieus of Boeotia.[83] They deliberately left a loose stone, a secret point of entry that they could enter to steal from the amassed wealth. Hyrieus, baffled at his depleting riches (though the keys and seals had not been tampered with), set a trap within the treasury. During their following heist, Agamedes was caught in the snare and unable to get free. Protecting his brother's identity, Trophonius cut off Agamedes' head, leaving behind an unrecognizable decapitated body. Suddenly the earth spontaneously opened up, swallowing Trophonius, and he was transformed from a man into a god. His chthonic cult was focused on the cave where he dwelled beneath the earth, located in Boeotia.

Classical sources describe the oracular process as conducted at night, commencing with the sacrifice of a ram into a pit sacred to Agamedes.[84] In days leading up to this, an individual was lodged within a small secluded dwelling where they were prescribed a preparatory diet of sacrificial meat, conducted preliminary prayers, abstained from sex and were allowed only to take cold river baths. Yulia Ustinova notes that these precursors essentially primed the person into an appropriate state: 'Only when well-prepared for the tremendous experience, that is, exhausted, tense with anticipation, and disposed to hallucinating, did the consulter descend to Trophonius' cave.'[85] Two boys dressed as Hermes escorted the person towards to Trophonius' cave, reflecting the divine winged messenger's function as Psychopompos, the guider of souls in the Underworld.[86] On the way, this initiate was made to drink from two rivers called Lethe and Mnemosyne, these being waters of the Underworld also mentioned on the Orphic gold tablets. A sacred image (which was apparently made by the mythological architect Daedalus, better known for designing the labyrinth that housed the minotaur) was displayed and then concealed.

The individual then made the long descent into the dark and cool grotto, carrying with them honey cakes to offer to snakes that dwelt at the bottom.[87] Within the depths of the

Earth unspeakable terrors were witnessed, so frightening that an individual returned unable to talk about what secret things they had seen. Thus 'To go down into the cave of Trophonius' became a well-known saying referring to suffering a great fright. The character Strepsiades in Aristophanes' comic play *The Clouds* remarks, 'I am afraid of descending within, as if into the cave of Trophonius,' when initiated by Socrates into a satirical religion based on veneration of thought.[88] On returning from the cave, the enquirer was seated upon the chair of Mnemosyne. There, priests composed an oracle based on that person's ravings about the startling experience.[89] During the surreal experience within the cave, Trophonius was alleged to manifest in terrifying awe before his enquirers and directly answer their questions. After such close interaction with the divine, a period of recuperation was apparently necessary. The family of a consultee was required to collect them immediately after the ritual, while they began to recover in all their faculties.

Plutarch provides a description of the climax at the bottom of the cave that was experienced by a certain Timarchus: 'He lay a long while upon the ground, but was not certain whether awake or in a dream, only he imagined that a smart stroke fell upon his head, and that through the parted sutures of his skull his soul fled out.'[90] In a whirling vision, Timarchus' soul soared over a vast glimmering ocean filled with islands. Timarchus is spoken to by a disembodied voice that gives a lengthy dialogue on the nature of the soul and its ability to transmigrate, predicting his understanding of this will be all the greater with his approaching death in three months' time. Timarchus comes to his senses with a violent headache, finding himself at the entrance of the cave. These Classical sources compare the oracle of Trophonius to a descent into Hades, with a return like that of Orpheus/Dionysus. Enveloping darkness was then followed by restored light. In experiencing a simulated death, a person learned that it was not to be feared.

SEVEN

GODS FROM ANATOLIA

Several of the mystery religions in Greece and Rome claimed gods originating from Asia Minor as their patrons. Most prominent among these was the cult of the Great Mother of the Gods, the *Magna Mater*. While there are multiple divine figures to whom this epithet was given,[1] she was most commonly identified as Cybele. Cybele was a goddess of mountains and wild animals. Much like the Dionysian Mysteries, her untamed rites were generally conducted in the forest. However, she could also play an important role in urban centres. On the advice of an oracle, she was brought to Rome as a religious ally against Carthage during the Second Punic War (218–201 BC). Her most sacred image, a large black stone that was said to have fallen from the sky (likely a meteorite), was removed from Cybele's principal cult centre in Phrygia and brought back to Rome.[2] On the way, the ship that carried the goddess' image apparently became stuck in a sandbar of the Tiber. A certain woman named Claudia Quinta, who had been accused of promiscuity, proved her virtue by calling upon the goddess's assistance, single-handedly pulling the ship free and then towing it with her sash to its destination.[3] Several sanctuaries to

Cybele are known from the Roman capital, including a major temple on the Palatine Hill and a shrine within the Circus Maximus.

In Classical art Cybele is usually portrayed seated with lions flanking either side of her throne, or being pulled in a lion-drawn chariot. She wears a round *polos*, or has her head fortified with a mural crown that bears the form of city

Marble statuette of the goddess Cybele, 1st–2nd century AD.

Bronze statuette of Cybele on a cart drawn by lions, 2nd century AD.

walls.[4] The goddess generally holds a tympanum drum in one hand and a *phiale* libation bowl in the other. Cybele appears to be derived from an earlier Bronze Age predecessor named Kubaba.[5] Neo-Hittite reliefs that depict this goddess portray her as similarly wearing a *polos* crown and holding two round objects – a pomegranate and a mirror.[6]

Cybele's priests, *korybantes*, guided followers into a state of joyous abandonment, dancing to the accompaniment of music produced by the tympanum, castanets, cymbals and flutes. Plato alludes to such worship when rebuffing two speakers in a debate who

> are doing the same thing as in the *teletai* of the *korybantes* when they perform the *thronesis* [enthronement] around a person who is to be initiated. For there is dancing and playing, as you know if you have been

> initiated. And now these two are simply performing a choral dance around you, so that afterwards they can initiate you.[7]

The condescending reference rather usefully alludes to how individuals were sat upon a throne (much like the goddess herself) during initiation while performers danced around them. Raucous theatrics of Cybele's worship also included a warrior dance performed by men clad in armour, who clashed their shields in rhythm. Cybele's priests asked for alms on her behalf, parading an icon of the goddess through civic areas to recruit new initiates.[8] They wore colourful robes, with images depicting Cybele and her lover Attis adorning their bodies.

Detail of the silver Parabiago Plate depicting lions pulling the chariot of Cybele and Attis, 4th century AD. Dancing Korybantes accompany their procession.

CYBELE AND ATTIS

Blood and gender-bending are central to the myths of Cybele.[9] The goddess's story begins with the birth of a deity named Agdistis who has both male and female strength, this being much feared by other gods.[10] A plan is devised whereby Dionysus spikes a water fountain with wine from which Agdistis drinks. After the drunken Agdistis has fallen asleep, Dionysus ties a rope to the hermaphrodite's male genitalia. Agdistis awakes, staggers and rips the penis from their body, unintentionally castrating themself. Blood from Agdistis' wound spills onto the earth, from which sprouts either a pomegranate or an almond tree. The myth is not entirely clear but it appears that, once castrated, Agdistis becomes Cybele; they are syncretized with and used as an epithet for the goddess.[11]

Sometime later, a maiden named Nana picks the pomegranate fruit (or almonds) of the plant, which she places in her lap. This impregnates her, the child conceived being Attis. Nana's disapproving father insists she exposes the child to the elements. Cybele saves the baby, putting Attis under the care of a she-goat. He grows up to become a shepherd, depicted in art as a youth who wears a Phrygian cap, wielding a crook and panpipes. Cybele adores her young paramour. She grooms him into her most devoted priest, but becomes jealous when he starts a relationship with another woman. The goddess inflicts him with madness, and in a state of frenzy he castrates himself under a pine tree by the river Gallus. There Attis dies from blood loss, much to the sorrow of Cybele. From his blood, violets spring up and entwine around the pine. The trunk of this tree is transported by Cybele to her cave. She circumambulates around the wooden icon in lamentation, wounding her breast in mourning.

A variant of this myth reports that the death resulted from a king of Phrygia's unrequited desire for Attis. Fighting off the unwanted sexual advances, Attis defends himself by emasculating the monarch. The king does the same to Attis, castrating the youth out of revenge as he himself lays dying from blood loss. Another account narrates that Attis bled to death after being wounded by a boar.[12] Attis is either turned into a pine tree, which becomes a symbol of the god, or in some versions has his body rendered immune to decomposition. In the latter, his hair keeps on growing and only his fingers are granted full immortality – they continue to move though he has perished.[13]

Relief from Saint-Bertrand-de-Comminges depicting the self-castration of Attis, 3rd century AD.

FESTIVAL AND FERVOUR

Cybele's cult had been established in Athens by the fifth century BC, with a temple to her known as the Metroon located in the agora, the thriving central business hub of the city.[14] Legend had it that this sanctuary was offered to placate the goddess, who had exacted a plague on Athens.[15] This pestilence apparently occurred after her itinerant priests (referred to as *metragyrtai*, 'beggars for the Mother') were martyred during an attempt to introduce Cybele's cult to Athens from the East. A festival known as the *Galaxia* was held in her honour, named after the barley porridge consumed by attendees.[16] But just how it was celebrated has not been preserved. More is known about a later Roman festival held annually for Cybele in March. The event opened with a presentation of cut reeds at her sanctuary, followed by several days of fasting and abstinence from sexual intercourse.[17] A freshly cut pine tree was then displayed, adorned with decorations that included purple flowers, ribbons and a depiction of Attis.[18]

A special class of Cybele's priests in the Roman era known as the *galli*, who were eunuch attendants of the goddess, are particularly associated with the next day of the festival. The *Dies Sanguinis* ('Day of Blood') was the traditional day of their self-castration, their devotion demonstrated in this extreme act.[19] In this, they identified with Attis and mourned his death.[20] The fervent *galli* also whipped themselves until they bled. After this intense spectacle came two days of rest and feasting. The festival concluded with the heavenly black stone of the Magna Mater being brought from her temple

Relief of archigallus offering sacrifice at an altar to Attis, 3rd century AD.
The image of the god stands beneath a pine tree.

on the Palatine and washed in a river just outside the city.[21] The *cista*, in which sacred objects of Cybele were concealed, may have served as a receptacle for preserved testicles of the castrated *galli*.[22] If this was the case, there may be a distorted truth preserved in Clement of Alexandria's hostile claim that the *cista* in the Bacchic mysteries contained a phallus. A marble three-dimensional representation of a *cista* from Ostia bears the inscription of an *archigallus* (chief priest of the *galli*) named Modius Maximus. Its form could also have been intended to evoke a modius grain measure, alluding both to fertility and the dedicator's name. It is topped with a cock ('gallus' in Latin).[23]

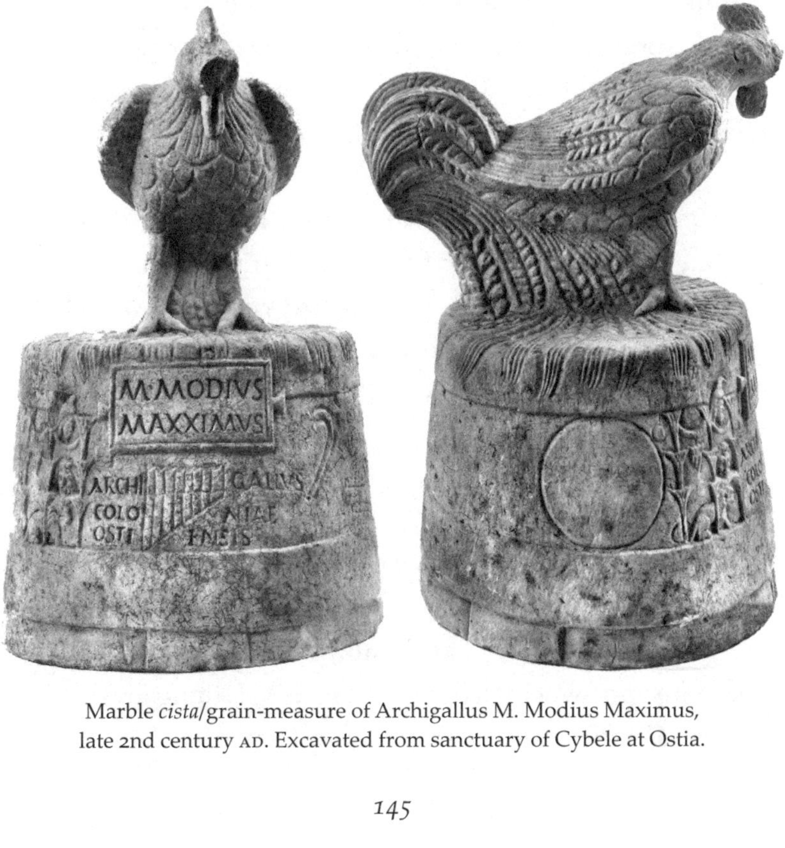

Marble *cista*/grain-measure of Archigallus M. Modius Maximus, late 2nd century AD. Excavated from sanctuary of Cybele at Ostia.

The *galli* seem to have occupied a third gender in the Roman world who transgressed traditional Roman conventions of masculinity. Their sacrificial emasculation, whereby they renounced their own fertility for the sake of the goddess, sat uncomfortably in Roman society. A *gallus* named Genucius was denied his inheritance in a legal case of the first century AD, as he 'had of his own accord allowed himself to be castrated and was not to be reckoned either a man or woman'.[24] The experience of the *galli* echoes that of modern transgender and nonbinary people, who similarly face discrimination for their defiance of birth gender. A poem by Catullus (first century BC) presents Attis as one of the *galli*, a 'counterfeit woman' who castrates himself and survives to become one of Cybele's followers. By the end of poem Attis regrets the act. The gender pronouns used to describe Attis change following his emasculation:

> He cut off his testicles with a sharp flint.
> She then, aware of her limbs without the man,
> While the ground was still spotted with fresh blood
> Quickly took in her snowy hands a tambourine
> Such serves your initiates, Cybele, instead of the
> trumpet
> And shaking the hollow calf-hide with delicate
> fingers
> Quivering, she began to sing . . .[25]

The *galli* appear to have embraced their status despite social disapproval by wearing women's clothing and accessories. This is seen in the elaborate dress worn by an *archigallus* on a marble funerary relief from Lavinium of the mid-second century AD. Firmicus Maternus (early fourth century AD) reports 'they say they are not men . . . they want to pass as women . . . priests who have womanish voices'.[26] Classicist Shelley Hales places the *galli* in context, that 'Greek and Roman literature consistently reinforces the sexual and racial difference of eunuchs by stressing how different they look. They were presented as wearing bright clothes, heavy jewellery, make-up and sporting bleached and crimped hair.'[27] Initially, the *galli* must have been foreigners and slaves, as castration was forbidden for Roman citizens. The emperor Claudius repealed this ban, although it was subsequently re-affirmed by Domitian.[28] Castration in Cybele's cult later became viewed as a symbolic spiritual act that was achieved by abstaining from sex.[29] A portion of a follower's soul was severed from their earthly body during the Mysteries and given to the heavenly goddess.

Another form of bloody sacrifice known as the taurobolium served as a purification ritual as part of initiation into Cybele's religion. Again, due to the cult's secrecy, it is poorly understood and the most notorious description of the practice comes from an unfriendly late Christian source. Prudentius (fourth century AD) describes it as a baptism by bull's blood, whereby an individual descends into a

> trench dug deep in the ground to be made holy . . . Above him they lay planks to make a stage . . . When the beast for sacrifice has been stationed here, they cut its breast open with a consecrated hunting-spear and the great wound disgorges a stream of hot blood,

> pouring on the plank-bridge below a steaming river which spreads billowing out. It passes in a shower, dripping a foul rain . . . getting his robe and his whole body covered with corruption.[30]

By taking this sanguine shower, the bovine life-energy is conferred onto the individual. Other epigraphic evidence suggests that the focus of taurbolia was the dedication of a sacrificed animal's testicles to Cybele, performed by both men and women.[31] This was perhaps a substitute for offering one's own testicles (an act that would otherwise be impossible for women), as not all could be as intense in their devotion as the *galli*. Taurobolium altars and taurobolic inscriptions of initiates indicate that they viewed the rite as an important moment of transition. Several state that after this experience the initiate was 'reborn' (*renatus*), while others refer to having conducted the Taurobolium on their (or as a new) 'birthday' (*natalicium*).[32] It is possible that this ritual changed over time, with some individuals opting for the more extreme form of a gory downpour.

SABAZIOS POINTS THE WAY

A curious type of object survives that appears to have had a ritualistic function in another cult that claimed a Phrygian deity as its patron. These are hands made of bronze, the principal archaeological evidence of the god Sabazios' worship during the Roman Empire. There are around eighty known examples of hands of Sabazios that have been found in military camps, as well as in domestic settings such as at

Bronze bust of Sabazios, 2nd century AD.

Pompeii.[33] Each is life-sized or slightly smaller. The hands are sculptured with the enigmatic decorations of various fauna, flora and other symbolic objects. Snakes frequently slither around the palms. Pine cones are often atop one of the fingers. On the wrist of some, a woman is depicted nursing a child within a semi-circular enclosure (perhaps a cave?). Cultic objects represented on the hands, from sacrificial knives to musical instruments, evoke the forgotten

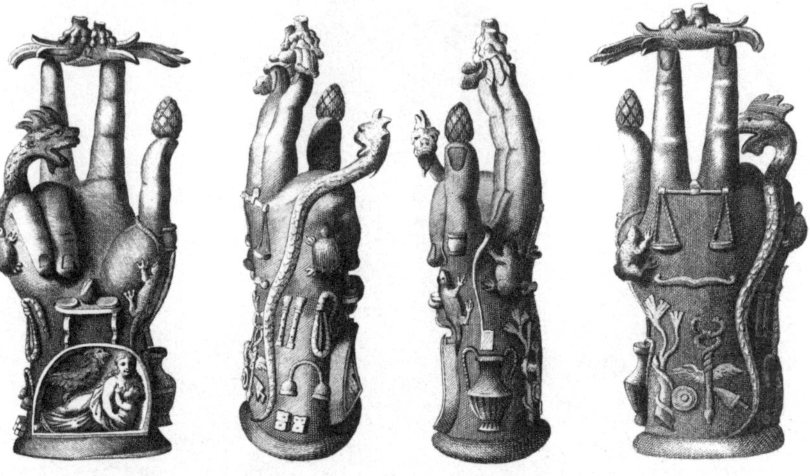

Line drawings depicting a hand of Sabazios from each side, illustrating the many symbols that cover its surface. In Giovanni Carafa di Noja's *Alcuni monumenti del Museo Carrafa* (1778).

rites of the god. An example in the Walters Art Museum even has an opening on its front. It was once covered by a hinged door, the unfastening of which would have revealed some now-lost sacred item concealed within its inner compartment.[34]

Sabazios was a divine horseman of the sky, and thus the bronze hands appropriately point heavenward. This is also reflected in the recurring image of a ladder on the hands, suggestive of ascent for the initiated. Moral expectations are hinted in the motif of a set of scales. Sabazios was also assigned chthonic attributes. Snakes, lizards and frogs that appear in the iconographic programme were regarded in the Classical world as regenerative animals who were in contact with the Underworld.[35] Each of the hands makes the *benedictio latina* sign with its thumb, index and middle finger raised.[36] The little finger and ring finger are closed into the palm. This gesture is still associated with bestowing blessing in Christianity. Their exact function is unknown, but it has been suggested that they may have been mounted on poles for use in cultic processions.[37] The eye-catching hands are truly mysterious objects, the exact significance of which was probably only understood by followers of Sabazios.

Bronze hand of Sabazios, 3rd century AD.
A hinged door once covered the opening on the wrist.
The unknown object stored within has not survived.

Marble sculpture of Glycon, 2nd century AD.

EIGHT

GLYCON; OR, HOW TO START YOUR OWN RELIGIOUS CULT IN ANTIQUITY

While many of the mystery religions, like that of Eleusis, had enduring origins that extended far back into the Bronze Age, new, smaller cults emerged sporadically across the Greco-Roman world that offered exclusive spiritual experiences. This provided an opportunity for charlatans, who were set on extracting wealth and renown from the gullible through invented religious schemes. These imitated and drew on existing elements known from established mystery cults. Adeimantus in Plato's *Republic* is dismissive of such

> itinerant priests and seers who go to rich men's doors and make them believe that they by means of sacrifices and incantations have accumulated a treasure of power from the gods that can expiate and cure with pleasurable festivals any misdeed of a man or his ancestors, and that if a man wishes to harm an enemy, at slight cost he will be enabled to injure just and unjust alike, since they are masters of spells and enchantments that constrain the gods to serve their end.[1]

Such suspicion is apparent in contemptuous statements about the *orpheotelestai* and other private initiators. There was a fine line between mystery cult and superstition. A figure like Apuleius, who liked being initiated in as many different systems as possible, could end up on trial for sorcery.

GLYCON

The best description of an apparent fraudster at work comes from the writings of Lucian of Samosata (second century AD). Lucian's satiric biography *Alexander the False Prophet* is still a highly amusing read for a modern audience, reporting on the cult founded by Alexander of Abonoteichus in the most scathing terms. This cult was based on veneration of a snake-god named Glycon, after Alexander had apparently been foretold of his coming by the medicinal deity Asclepius. Lucian reports that in a temple at Chalcedon, Alexander planted an ancient-looking tablet with text that proclaimed Abonoteichus (of the Paphlagonia Region on the Black Sea in what is now modern Turkey) to be the location for the appearance of a new Asclepius. He had apparently picked his hometown for the ruse, with his knowledge that its people were wealthy, stupid and superstitious. The citizens of Abonoteichus enthusiastically began work on a new sanctuary in anticipation of the coming divine epiphany. Alexander returned to the city, bringing with him a particularly docile species of snake from Macedonia. These serpents were so well domesticated that apparently people had them as pets in that country, and even allowed them to sleep in bed with children.

According to Lucian, Alexander placed a small live snake within an emptied goose egg and sealed it with wax. He then hid the egg within the foundations of the temple that was under construction. As the god's prophet, Alexander drew a crowd to subsequently witness the 'birth' of this new Asclepius. Taking the tiny creature home for a few days, he replaced it with one of the aforementioned (full-sized) Macedonian serpents to imply it had grown at record speed. Wrapping the snake around his body and attaching to it a mechanical humanoid head operated with puppetry, Alexander founded a religion that featured three main elements: oracular pronouncements, healing rituals and mysteries that provided secret knowledge to the initiated. Confinement of space, restriction of time and reduced lighting created the effect in

> a little room, not very bright and not admitting too much daylight. Enters a crowd of heterogeneous humanity, excited, wonder-struck in advance, agog with hopes. When they went in, the thing, of course, seemed to them a miracle . . . and before they could look closely, they were forced out, were immediately crowded towards the exit, by those who kept coming in, for another door had been opened on the opposite side as an exit.[2]

Entwined around its prophet in a dark torchlit chamber, the speaking snake declared its name was Glycon ('sweet one').

Glycon's mysteries were revealed over the course of a three-day rite. The first day celebrated the births of Apollo and his son Asclepius. Day two was in homage to the arrival of Glycon. On the third day, Alexander's own birth and that of his daughter were commemorated. In a re-enactment of the latter, Alexander apparently played himself. A woman adopted the persona of the Moon-goddess, who he claimed had mothered his child. As Alexander lay in feigned sleep below, she dramatically flew down from the temple roof as though descending from the heavens. Lucian reports that many deluded women (with the support of their husbands) had sex with Alexander under the belief they were lying with the god. There is a contemporary inscription that may attest to this practice, referring to a priest from Paphlagonia who was named as Miletos, son of Glycon.[3] Lucian reports that during the mystic ceremonies Alexander made sure to expose his legs so that his 'golden thigh' would glint in the torch-light. This attempt at imitating the golden thigh of Pythagoras was a gilded piece of leather affixed to his leg. 'Hail Glycon,' he proclaimed, to which initiates responded, 'Hail Alexander.'[4]

The cult brought Alexander prestige and he amassed wealth from the fees required of worshippers. He arranged for the marriage of his half-lunar daughter to the proconsul of Asia. During the Antonine Plague an oracular verse of Glycon was disseminated across the empire, to be hung above gateways for protection. Lucian reports that houses marked with the inscription actually ended up being those most afflicted with illness. Even the emperor Marcus Aurelius sought out the prophecies of Glycon. But though he was told that throwing two lions into the Danube would secure a military victory, the army was met with a disastrous defeat against a Germanic people known as the Marcomanni.

Lucian's hatred of Alexander emerges in his hilarious yet highly biased biography. When they met, Lucian claims to have greeted Alexander by biting his hand. Having set many a trap to expose the fraud, Lucian reports that the prophet attempted to murder him. Lucian's account closes with the death of Alexander, which was rather unheroically caused by a gangrenous leg.

With its ability to renew itself by the shedding of its skin, the snake had long been venerated in the Mediterranean as a symbol of wisdom, healing and resurrection. This new religious movement drew influence from the well-established cult of the medicinal god Asclepius. His major sanctuary was at Epidauros, with another important Asclepieion located at Pergamon.[5] It was a serpent who first taught Asclepius his healing arts, and the god's snake-entwined staff remains a symbol of medicine today. A notable feature of his cult was incubation, in which patients would sleep in his temple in the hope of being visited at night by the god, who would reveal cures for illnesses in dreams.[6] Pergamon came to produce a type of coinage known as the *cistophorus*,[7] which featured the distinct motif of a snake emerging from a *cista*, the box used for concealing the sacred objects in the mystery religions we have discussed.

Images of Glycon appear on Roman imperial coins. Bronze currency from Abonoteichos, struck during the reign of Antoninus Pius (emperor from AD 138 to 161), features the head of the ruler on one side and the divine serpent on the reverse. A unique marble statue of Glycon that dates from the late second century was discovered during excavations in Constanța (known in ancient times as Tomi), Romania.

The 66-centimetre-high (26 in.) sculpture has human ears and a head of long, human hair, with its coiled, scaly body sitting upon a circular base. Several smaller bronze statuettes of the god survive, including an example found at the Athenian Agora. The cult declined after the death of its charismatic leader in circa AD 170. Its survival for about one hundred years after Alexander's passing reflects the pre-existing association of snakes with healing rituals conducted around the Mediterranean.

ELAGABAL

Even more threatening than a new cult was the introduction of a new Eastern religion by the emperor himself. One god associated with mysteries was almost promoted to the chief god of Rome. This was the Syrian solar deity Elagabal, venerated by Roman emperor Marcus Aurelius Antoninus. He is better known as Heliogabalus or Elagabalus, names posthumously given to him after that of his god. Heliogabalus grew up in Emesa, Syria, where his family held high positions in the priesthood of Elagabal. He became the emperor as a teenager in AD 218 through a military coup arranged by his grandmother Julia Maesa.[8] Shortly after moving to the capital, Heliogabalus also had the local god brought to Rome. Elagabal did not have a cult statue, the god taking the form of a conical black stone. Coins depicting Elagabal show an eagle with wings spread over the baetyl, likely a coverlet that concealed the god beneath. Contemporary historian Herodian (*c.* AD 170–240) disapprovingly describes Elagabal: 'This stone is worshipped as though it were sent from heaven;

on it there are some small projecting pieces and markings that are pointed out, which the people would like to believe are a rough picture of the sun, because this is how they see them.'[9] Visual evidence from numismatics sometimes depicts the stone as being marked with stars on its surface. It is most likely that Elagabal, whose name is of Semitic origin and means God of the Mountain, was a meteorite that fell from the sky.[10] In Rome he was assimilated with the sun god as Sol Invictus Elagabal. A temple known as the Elagabalium was constructed as the home for the sacred stone. The emperor arranged a marriage for Elagabal, having the image of a goddess taken from Carthage to join the solar deity in Rome as his wife.[11]

In festivities in honour of the god, Heliogabalus had the sacred stone paraded through Rome in a gold chariot, the carriage encrusted with jewels and pulled by six horses.[12] Apparently, there was no driver seat in the vehicle to guide its reins. This gave the impression that Elagabal himself was the charioteer. The emperor, dressed in his Eastern priestly robes, ran backwards holding the reigns ahead of the chariot. He maintained constant eye contact, his reverential gaze fixed on his god. Sacrifices of sheep and cows to Elagabal were conducted at dawn. Pigs were unsuitable, as the consumption of pork was forbidden by the cult.[13] The emperor apparently compelled disgruntled senators to watch as he danced around Elagabal's altar, accompanied by orgiastic music from drums, flutes and cymbals. These displays resemble the civic processions we have encountered in the cults of Cybele and Dionysus. The less public aspects of his worship are unknown, although the *Historia Augusta* (*c.* fourth century AD) reports that the emperor appropriated hallowed images and rituals of various other cults to the Elagabalium. To the temple of his god, Heliogabalus sought to

> transfer the emblem of the Great Mother, the fire of Vesta, the Palladium, the shields of the Salii, and all that the Romans held sacred, purposing that no god might be worshipped at Rome save only Elagabal. He declared, furthermore, that the religions of the Jews and the Samaritans and the rites of the Christians must also be transferred to this place, in order that the priesthood of Elagabal might include the mysteries of every form of worship.[14]

The intention was not to abolish these cults, but rather provide access to the secrets of all religions for both Elagabal and his priesthood.[15]

Other lurid tales circulated that human sacrifice was apparently practised in the temple of Elagabal.[16] Such rumours about his religious policy (even if they were exaggerated or completely invented) no doubt contributed to his wider unpopularity in Rome. Among his negatively received secular habits were opulent displays of wealth, non-heteronormative sexual behaviour and jokes made in poor taste (sometimes quite literally). The emperor was known for hosting elaborate feasts. But it was never certain whether diners were in for a trick or a treat. Heliogabalus was reputed to serve hungry guests multi-course dinners of inedible painted images of meals or models of food rendered in materials such as wax, wood, marble, ivory, terracotta or glass.[17] In a display evocative of modern performance art, he held banquets in which all food served was a single colour – green one day and blue the next.[18] After a short reign, Heliogabalus was assassinated in AD 222. The meteoritic god was sent back to Emesa in the principate of his successor and the temple on the Palatine rededicated to Jupiter. While some Roman provinces had adopted worship of the god, this also quickly faded.

These two episodes illustrate attempts at introducing new cults that did not last beyond the demise of their charismatic leaders. They faced similar suspicion and opposition to other mystery experiences we have examined that were perceived to have originated in the East. But in the third and fourth centuries another religion was gaining followers. Those who were initiated into this cult, however, were required to worship its one God exclusively. With the rise of Christianity came the decline of polytheistic mystery experiences produced in the Greco-Roman world.

The iconography of Isis suckling Horus was influential on the development of imagery of the Madonna nursing the Christ Child. Small faience statuette, 332–330 BC.

NINE

FROM EARLY CHRISTIANITY TO MODERNITY

At the end of the fourth century AD, pagan worship was banned by the Roman emperor Theodosius. By this stage, prominent sites of mystery worship like Eleusis had been sacked and were never rebuilt. Mithraea around the empire suffered Christian vandalization or in some cases were abandoned completely intact. Though this was the end of the Classical mystery religions, remnants of their practices found continuity in late antiquity and are still evoked today.

CHRISTIANITY: A MYSTERY RELIGION?

A popular proposal in nineteenth- and twentieth-century scholarship was the idea that Christianity began as a mystery religion, and was the only one ultimately to survive antiquity. One of those who wrote on the subject was Martin Luther King Jr. Better known for his activism during the civil rights movement, he addressed the topic in a paper from 1950 titled 'The Influence of the Mystery Religions on Christianity'. As a student of theology, he also penned the article 'A Study of Mithraism' (1949).[1] Christianity's offering of salvation likely appealed to initiates of the established mystery cults.

We have met multiple dying and resurrecting gods. Christ in the New Testament is likewise presented as a rising fertility god who like a solar deity is identified as a source of light.[2] Mithraism in particular was perceived by scholars to be both a rival to Christianity and influential on its development in late antiquity. But while ritual aspects of Christianity may resemble those in mystery religions – such as purificatory initiation via baptism and the shared meal of the Eucharist – these were not exclusive to the practices of the cults discussed. Rituals in Judaism and the wider ancient religious milieu are more likely sources of inspiration.

That said, sacraments in early Christianity were sometimes referred to by the term *mysterion* and were not to be discussed with those outside the religion.[3] The late fifth-century AD *Ecclesiastical Hierarchy* of Pseudo-Dionysius proclaims, 'Let your respect for the things of the hidden God be shown in knowledge that comes from the intellect and is unseen. Keep these things of God unshared and undefiled by the uninitiated.'[4] To the non-initiated, Christian rites had long been regarded with secrecy. This led at times to Christian practices being wildly misunderstood. Marcus Minucius Felix (third century AD) rather memorably records the misinterpretation of holy communion, a shared meal of bread and wine as symbols of Christ's body and blood, as cannibalism:

> Now the story about the initiation of young novices is as much to be detested as it is well known. An infant covered over with meal, that it may deceive the unwary, is placed before him who is to be stained

> with their rites: this infant is slain by the young pupil, who has been urged on as if to harmless blows on the surface of the meal, with dark and secret wounds. Thirstily – Oh the horror! – they lick up its blood. Eagerly they divide the limbs. By this victim they are pledged together; with this consciousness of wickedness they are covenanted to mutual silence. Such sacred rites as these are more foul than any sacrileges . . .[5]

Its misunderstanding of the sacred is strikingly similar to Christian sources discussed in earlier chapters, which did the same in their perversion of the Mysteries. Such references to secret knowledge shared by Christians were the result of the persecution they initially faced. But early Christianity was a much more inclusive religion, with the mission of Jesus Christ being to reveal God's mysteries to all.[6] There were no expensive Isiac initiations or Mithraic exclusions of female participants. Nor was there anything like the threat of capital punishment for divulging secrets of Eleusis, with Christianity instead openly proclaiming its message.

The influence of the Mysteries on Christian ritual practice is still a matter of debate. But whatever the case, early Christian imagery certainly borrowed from the iconography found in mystery cults and broader Greco-Roman religion. This assimilation of images is apparent in adaption of the iconography of Isis suckling Horus into the icon of the Virgin Mary with baby Jesus. The epithet *Stella Maris* ('Star of the Sea') used to praise the seafaring function of Classical Isis was also inherited as a title for the Madonna.[7] Mary likewise shares with Isis the title *Regina Caeli* ('Queen of Heaven'). Similar adoption of motifs is found in one of the earliest surviving depictions of Jesus, the Hinton St Mary Mosaic (fourth century AD). The unconventional halo that crowns the bust of Christ takes the form of a Chi-Rho and two pomegranates that surround his head. Use of the fruit instantly evokes Persephone, a goddess who died and was reborn and whose Eleusinian mysteries offered a salvation to initiates. The image of dying wheat and its resurrection in John 12:24 recalls her mourning mother Demeter. The reuse of such familiar motifs would make conversion to Christianity an easier process.

Other comparisons are found in the writings of the early Christian writer Justin Martyr (second century AD). He relates the pagan beliefs that Dionysus was the son of a

Roundel mosaic of Christ from Hinton St Mary, early 4th century AD. Jesus adopts pomegranates as a symbol of his resurrection from Persephone.

divine king, that wine was used in his mysteries and that he was dismembered and then ascended into the heavens.[8] Christianity provided the 'true' meaning behind concepts imitated by these false gods. The Hellenistic Jewish philosopher Philo of Alexandria (*c.* 20 BC–AD 50) draws a similar comparison when discussing the consumption of wine in Jewish mysticism by those 'having drunk as in the Bacchic rites of the strong wine of God's love'.[9] The emotion felt by mystics in both Christianity and Judaism contains some of the ecstatic behaviour we have encountered in mystery religions. Such loss of self that could be experienced in religious ecstasy is most famously captured in Gian Lorenzo Bernini's sculpture of the sixteenth-century St Teresa of Avila. The term 'mysteries' in Christianity today departs from its use in ancient Greco-Roman religion. It refers instead to miraculous aspects of Christian theology that cannot be explained, such as the virgin birth of Jesus and the nature of the Trinity.

BEING A *MYSTES* IN THE MODERN WORLD

Initiation remains an important aspect of defining communities today. Rituals performed within certain groups are notable for their similarities to ancient Greco-Roman Mystery religions. Mithraism is often compared with the fraternal organization of Freemasonry.[10] Both feature ritual use of blindfolds, advancing degrees of initiation and the sharing of secret knowledge on the meaning that lies behind esoteric symbols. As a Masonic lodge uses imagery and architecture to evoke the Temple of Solomon, so too does a Mithraeum recreate the Mithraic cave. Parallels have similarly been noted between ecstatic dance involving snakes in the cult of Dionysus and modern serpent-handling Pentecostal churches that are found in the Appalachian region of the USA.[11] Neo-paganism has seen revival of the worship directed to many of the divine personalities revered in the Mystery cults. The fertility figures like Isis, Dionysus, Demeter and Persephone are especially popular veneration choices. An interesting exception, largely ignored in modern worship, is Mithras. The Classicist Andrew Fear succinctly provides the reason for this: 'Such neglect can be explained by the fact that Mithras, the soldier's god, has normally appealed to the socially conservative . . . while neopaganism tends to sit on the left side of politics.'[12]

Speaking from personal experience, the closest this author has come to the awe-struck, disorientating accounts of initiation into the Greco-Roman mysteries comes from a more profane example. The world of modern fitness contains much cultish behaviour. I have dabbled as a regular attendee of a spin class. In a low-lit room, illuminated only by UV blacklights, stripes of colour on our ritual garments (activewear) become bright. Some of us may have had a preparatory *kykeon*, the strange potion that is a pre-workout beverage. Upon a stationary bicycle we perform repetitions of various movements to the accompaniment of loud music. As a group we transition between agile motion on a light resistance and slow strained revolutions on a heavier load. Sweaty libations are poured towards the fitness goddess who provides instruction on an elevated podium at the front of the room. The exertion of the exercise is torturous, and yet hormonal release triggers a feeling of pure bliss at the end of a class. Sometimes I experience an out-of-body sensation while cycling. Closing my eyes deep into a class, I lose cognizance of the setting. The music penetrates my being and vivid imagery manifests in my mind's eye. While there is no requirement of secrecy (other than some reluctance to admit my hobby to respectable colleagues), there is very much a contrast between participants who understand the appeal and those outside the gym to whom the sober 6 a.m. disco on a stationary bike sounds absurd. Modern rave culture has similarly been noted for its ability to create an ecstatic environment.[13] There is a certain religiosity felt by those initiated into this type of partying: the combination of loud repetitive music, flashing neon lights and hypnotic dance (that may be bolstered with the taking of drugs) results in a transcendental experience for attendees.

Mystery religions sometimes feature in today's arts and pop culture representations of ancient Greece and Rome. An example is Ubisoft's 2018 role-playing video game *Assassin's Creed Odyssey*, which is set in Greece during the Peloponnesian War (431–404 BC). One side quest in the game features the parodic 'Mysteries of Hedone'. To be initiated the player is instructed to 'climb to the top of the Waterfall of Eternal Joy and dive into Froth of Fantasy . . . Then, explore the Cave of Deepest Self Knowledge and return with the treasure you'll find inside.' The game also features several sites mentioned in this book, the player roaming around ancient Greece being able to visit the Telesterion of Eleusis and descend into the cave of Trophonius.

Rudyard Kipling published the short poem 'A Song to Mithras' in 1906. Giving it a subordinate title of 'Hymn of the 30th Legion: Circa 350 AD', Kipling places his homage to the god in the mouths of Roman soldiers stationed on Hadrian's Wall. Each verse is set at a different time of day, tracking the movement of Mithras as a sun god across the sky. His sacrifice of the bull occurs in the final stanza at midnight. Its text was remixed in the 1998 song 'Lord of Ages' by the band Blood Axis. To the martial beat of a drum, the experimental Neofolk song employs lyrics from Kipling ('Mithras, God of the Morning, our trumpets waken the Wall! Rome is above the Nations, but Thou art over all!') in combination with ancient inscriptions from Mithraea ('Accept oh holy Father, accept the incense-burning Lions, Through whom we ourselves are consumed').[14]

The extremes of Dionysian ritual are evoked in Donna Tartt's 1992 novel *The Secret History*. It revolves around a group of college students in Vermont who, inspired by their studies of ancient Greece, attempt to reach a state of Dionysiac madness. While use of deprivation, alcohol and drugs to fuel their bacchanal eventually does cause the characters to completely lose awareness of themselves, they kill a man in the process. The shared secrecy consumes the group for the rest of this book, which drew inspiration from Euripides' *The Bacchae*.

Dionysian indulgence can be roused less murderously by gourmands, the god often evoked in marketing of modern fine dining. The restaurant Bacchanalia opened in London at the end of 2022. Its fantastical interiors are dominated by Damien Hirst sculptures of mythological figures, Classical-themed murals painted by Gary Myatt and the display of actual Greco-Roman antiquities. One can be initiated into

Bacchanalia's discreet and exclusive members club, limited to a maximum of five hundred people. Applicants are asked their occupation and interests, the cost being an eye-watering £5,000 annually (plus an additional joining fee of £1,750) at the time of writing.[15] I think Lucius of *The Golden Ass* would sympathize, given his exasperations at the ever-increasing initiation costs required by Isis.

The cult of Isis has frequently been referenced in modern works of fiction to evoke the mystique of Egypt, a classic example being the eighteenth-century fantasy novel *Life of Sethos* by Jean Terrasson. The author claimed that he had translated the book from an actual ancient Greek text, adopting a convention often used in ancient and medieval literature to give a work authority. The protagonist Sethos is initiated by Isis into her Mysteries in a scene that draws inspiration from *The Golden Ass* of Apuleius. The ceremony is conducted in a chamber hidden beneath the Great Pyramid of Giza and involves a series of trials that recall the Classical elements: a fiery run over hot metal bars, swinging through the air over a vast chasm and swimming a channel of water. The novel was influential on Wolfgang Amadeus Mozart's opera *The Magic Flute*, in which the character Tamino undergoes a series of ordeals conducted by priests of Isis and Osiris.

The mythology of Eleusis that revolves around Demeter and Persephone has likewise proven highly adaptable. The *Matrix* film trilogy is rich in allusions to ritual, religion and myth. The training of Neo resembles an initiation in which he must jump from building to building – a trial he initially fails. Explicit reference is found in the character of Persephone.

She provides access to the Keymaker, who can open a door to the Source (a heavenly central computing core).

Influenced by the ancient practice, British occultist Aleister Crowley (1875–1947) penned *The Rites of Eleusis*. This series of rituals focuses on the seven Classical planets, culminating in the final Rite of Saturn, which explored themes of mortality, time and transformation.[16] Most innovative is a piscatorial reworking of the Eleusis myth by Kim Antieau that 'updates the tale for modern sensibilities through the life cycle of a most remarkable creature: the salmon'.[17] Her 2001 book *The Salmon Mysteries: A Guidebook to a Reimagining of the Eleusinian Mysteries* retells the story of Demeter as a Native American animal legend, followed by instructions for performing a nine-day ecological-focused ceremony.

By virtue of their secrecy, we will never fully understand the mystery religions of Classical antiquity. But in the surviving evidence that has been examined in this book, we can see that a common theme of initiate experience was the overcoming of ignorance. Hidden truths were revealed. Mystery rituals were rich in symbolism, providing initiates with exclusive knowledge to achieve an elevated state of contact with the divine. Light and darkness, sound and silence, consumption of certain victuals and fasting, as well as movement (often to the point of exhaustion) were all used in creating these intense experiences. As Yulia Ustinova notes, this play on the senses primed individuals for entering an altered state of conscious in which 'Seeing the sacred symbols, even if they were in fact the most trivial objects, could then be perceived as a life-changing experience.'[18] These overwhelming encounters purified the body and mind. In exchange for financial and physical costs, they provided a more personal relationship with the divine. Some mystery initiations were intense one-off experiences, while others involved rituals that were regularly repeated. The rites could be anchored to a specific place such as at Samothrace or Eleusis. Alternatively they could be administered by travelling priests as in the case of Dionysus or Cybele. Sacred narratives were re-enacted in the Mysteries (such as Demeter's search for Persephone) and ritual spaces recreated mythological locations (like the Mithraic cave). Imitation of deeds performed by a god perhaps enabled the initiate to identify with and experience a sense of union with the divine. Secret knowledge provided to initiates had a powerful social benefit, creating a sense of group identity that contrasted with the ignorance of non-initiates. The Mysteries enhanced their lives with meaning and may have even prepared an individual for the next life.

GLOSSARY OF GODS AND HEROES IN THE MYSTERIES

Agdistis: Anatolian deity with both male and female characteristics associated with the cult of Cybele.

Aion: A god of time. He was proposed as a potential identification for the Leontocephaline figure found in Mithraic iconography.

Antinous: Lover of the Roman emperor Hadrian who lived AD 110–130. After drowning while in Egypt, the youth was deified and frequently compared to the god Osiris.

Anubis: Jackal-headed Egyptian god of mummification. As the deity who escorted souls in the afterlife, he was equated with Hermes/Mercury, the Psychopompos of the Classical world.

Aphrodite (Venus): Goddess of love who is commonly depicted naked in Classical art. She was syncretized with Isis in a form that emphasized the fertility aspect of the imported Egyptian goddess.

Apollo: Multifaceted god whose prerogatives included archery, music, light and prophecy. He is the brother of Artemis and father of Asclepius.

Artemis (Diana): Virgin goddess of wilderness and the hunt. Usually depicted wielding a bow and accompanied by a deer or hunting dogs, her cult at Ephesus venerated a distinct many-breasted form of the goddess.

Asclepius: God of medicine whose major healing sanctuaries were based at Pergamon and Epidauros. He is associated with snakes and incubation, and the practice of sleeping in the temple of a god was a major feature of his cult.

Athena (Minerva): Virgin daughter of Zeus, born from his head. This goddess of warfare and wisdom was the patron of Athens. She usually wears a warrior's helmet and her aegis breastplate crafted from the head of Medusa. Olives and owls are sacred to her.

Attis: Youthful lover of the goddess Cybele. Castrating himself for the Great Mother, he became a Phrygian vegetation deity. The priests known as *galli* replicated this act of devotion in Cybele's cult. Attis is associated with pine trees.

Castor and Pollux (Polydeuces): Twin brothers known collectively as the Dioscuri, who form the constellation Gemini. They are possible candidates for the mysterious collective of gods known as Kabeiroi.

Cautes and Cautopates: Twin attendants of Mithras that likely personify sunrise and sunset. Cautes holds a torch upright, while Cautopates points his downward with its flame inverted.

Cybele: Anatolian goddess identified as the Magna Mater who was associated with fertility. In art she is identifiable by her crown that bears the form of city walls and often holds instruments such as the tympanum used for producing the orgiastic music of her cult. Cybele is attended by lions, who flank her throne or pull her chariot. Her religious personnel included the shield-banging *korybantes*, self-castrated *galli* and alms-begging *metragyrtai*.

Demeter (Ceres): Olympian goddess of agriculture and mother of Persephone. She is the principle goddess of the Eleusinian Mysteries. Wheat, pigs and torches (with which she searched for her daughter) are her prerogative symbols. Mythology in the region of Arcadia saw her as mother to a second daughter identified as Despoina.

Demophoön: Prince of Eleusis and son of King Celeus and Queen Metanira. In the foundational myth of the Eleusinian Mysteries, he is nursed by Demeter. Her attempts to transform the baby into a god by roasting him in a divine fire are interrupted by his mother. He is not to be confused with his brother Triptolemus.

Despoina: Goddess whose name is unknown, referred to by this title meaning 'The Mistress'. She is the daughter of Demeter and Poseidon, both having adopted equine form at the time of her conception. Wild animals and animal-headed figures are associated with her cult.

Dionysus (Bacchus, Liber): God of wine, drama and divine-inspired madness. Grapes, ivy, theatrical masks and the thyrsus staff are his symbols. Dionysus' followers were the frenzied female maenads and half-goat satyrs. In myth he is born multiple times: retrieved from the burnt remains of his mother's body, brought to term in Zeus' thigh, and resurrected after being eaten by the Titans. Having rescued his mother Semele from the Underworld after death and overseeing her transformation into a goddess, he was believed to have special knowledge of the afterlife as reflected in one of his epithets: *Eleutherios* ('liberator').

Elagabal: Local Syrian sun god venerated in the form of a black stone that had fallen from the heavens (most likely a meteorite). He was promoted by the Roman emperor Marcus Aurelius Antoninus, who is better known today as Elagabalus or Heliogabalus after this religious policy.

Erinyes (Eumenides): The Furies, chthonic goddesses of retribution who pursued mortals guilty of crimes such as homicide and the breaking of oaths.

Glycon: Snake god promoted by Alexander of Abonoteichus. His cult drew heavy influence from that of Asclepius. Lucian of Samosata claims this new religion to be a hoax concocted by Alexander for fame and fortune.

Hades (Pluto): King of the Underworld. Though he initially abducted his wife Persephone, she came to rule as her husband's equal and took her role as Queen of the Underworld seriously. His three-headed dog Cerberus guarded the gates of the Underworld to prevent the dead from escaping. Though feared, he was not evil, and (despite frequently being portrayed as such in modern time) should not be seen as a figure comparable to Satan ruling in Hell.

Harmonia: Goddess from Samothrace, who left the island when she married Cadmus. She is well known for her ill-fated necklace received as a wedding gift that cursed its subsequent owners with misfortune.

Harpocrates: Classical version of the Egyptian god Horus, son of Isis and Osiris. He is often portrayed with his finger held to his lips and is associated with secrets. Images of Harpocrates/Horus on the lap of Isis were likely inspiration in the development of iconography of the Madonna nursing the Christ Child.

Hekate: Goddess of crossroads and magic. In sculpture, she is often depicted with three bodies facing different directions. Hekate assisted Demeter in the search for Persephone, guiding her path with flaming torches.

Helios (Sol): God of the Sun, who guided his solar chariot across the sky each day, and brother of the moon goddess, Selene/Luna. A halo or radiate crown often adorns his head. An important aspect of the god in the Roman world was *Sol Invictus* ('the unconquering sun'). Sol played a major role in Mithraism as both companion and an aspect of its titular god.

Hera (Juno): Queen of the gods, who was patron of marriage and protector of women in childbirth. The major cult centres for the wife of Zeus were based at Samos and Argos. The chryselephantine cult statue of the Argive Hera held a pomegranate, of which Pausanias (2.17.4) said he 'must say nothing, for its story is a holy mystery'.

Hermes (Mercury): Messenger of the gods, as well as the deity of travellers, thieves and commerce. Hermes is notable in the Mysteries as the Psychopompos ('guider of souls') who assists the newly dead by safely escorting them through to the perilous Underworld. As a god who crosses boundaries, he is associated with the type of boundary marker known as a herm, a marble pillar topped with a bust and sporting a phallus. Hermes is easily identified by the symbols he wears/wields: his winged sandals, caduceus staff and traveller's cap.

Iakkhos: God who personified the ritual shout 'iacche' of Eleusinian initiates as they paraded along the Sacred Way. He is sometimes identified as an aspect of Dionysus.

Isis: Egyptian goddess who was later imported into the Classical world as a patron of mysteries. She resurrected her husband Osiris (who came to be replaced by the composite god Serapis) and was the mother of Horus (later rebranded as Harpocrates). Symbols of her cult include the musical sistrum, garments tied with an Isis knot and the situla that was used for carrying purificatory Nile water. Her epithets included *Regina Caeli* (Queen of Heaven), and as a goddess who protected seafarers she was the *Stella Maris* (Star of the Sea).

Kabeiroi (Cabeiri): Group of deities worshipped on Samothrace, though the term *Theoi Megaloi* (Great Gods) is more commonly used. Although the individual gods that made up the collective have been variously and contradictorily identified in ancient sources, it is possible that they were intentionally ambiguous shadowy figures. Cult centres for the Kabeiroi were also present on Lemnos and in Boeotian Thebes.

Lethe: Goddess who personified forgetfulness/oblivion. Lethe was also one of the rivers of the Underworld that caused those who drank from it to forget their life experiences. The gold tablets associated with the Bacchic-Orphic mysteries warn initiates against drinking from the waters of Lethe, and to instead quench their thirst from the river Mnemosyne.

Mithras: Roman god of mysteries who was believed to come from Persia, though he bore little resemblance to his Iranian namesake. Imagery depicting his slaying of a celestial bull (known as the Tauroctony) was replicated in each Mithraea, the small cave-temples of his cult. He is associated with light and astrological imagery, the solar aspect of the god reflected in his full title *Deus Sol Invictus Mithras*. Particularly popular with the Roman army, initiation into Mithraism appears to have been restricted to men only.

Mnemosyne: Goddess of memory and mother of the nine Muses. A pool sacred to Mnemosyne was a geographic feature of the Underworld. The Orphic-Bacchic gold tablets instruct the dead to drink from these waters instead of the amnesic river of Lethe.

Nike (Victoria): Personification of Victory. The winged goddess descended from the heavens to crown victorious individuals (be they of athletics, war or the arts) with wreaths.

Orpheus: Hero famed for his ability to sing and play the lyre. His mother was Calliope, the Muse of epic poetry. Orpheus descended to the Underworld in an attempt to retrieve his wife Eurydice. Hades and Persephone, moved by the poet's song, allowed for the release of Eurydice on the condition that Orpheus was to walk in front and not look back at her until once again in the land of the living. Orpheus forgets this stipulation as they make their ascent and loses his chance at resurrecting his love. Though unsuccessful, the experience gave him knowledge of the afterlife, imparting this secret information in mystery texts he was alleged to have composed.

Osiris: Fertility god and king of the Egyptian afterlife. He was killed by his brother Seth and resurrected through the process of mummification by his wife Isis. In the Greco-Roman world, he was often replaced by a new deity called Serapis who was made up of a combination of Classical and Egyptian elements.

Penates: Roman household gods associated with the hearth. Mythological tradition held that the original Penates were first brought from Samothrace to Troy and subsequently were carried by Aeneas to Italy.

Pentheus: Mythological King of Thebes who denied the spread of Dionysian worship in his city. He is punished for this hubris: the Theban women are driven into a state of madness and kill the king, tearing Pentheus limb from limb.

Persephone (Proserpina, Kore): Queen of the Underworld, daughter of Demeter and wife of Hades. The story of her abduction to the land of the dead and annual resurrection at springtime was central to the Eleusinian Mysteries. Her symbols include the pomegranate (which she consumed in the Underworld) and torches (which aided the search for the missing goddess).

Poseidon (Neptune): Trident-wielding god of the sea who was also associated with earthquakes and horses. Though his usual consort was Amphitrite, he fathered the mystery goddess Despoina with Demeter.

Sabazios: Phrygian horse-riding sky god. His cult is archaeologically attested by a unique type of ritual artefact. These are the bronze hands of Sabazios that make the *benedictio latina* gesture and are covered in mysterious symbols.

Selene (Luna): Goddess who personified the Moon. Her brother was the sun god Helios/Sol. Often crowned with a crescent on her forehead, she drives her moon chariot across the night sky.

Semele (Thyone): Daughter of Cadmus and Harmonia and mother of Dionysus. Semele was incinerated on seeing the terrifying true form of her lover Zeus. She was later rescued from the Underworld by Dionysus, who then oversaw her apotheosis from mortal into a goddess.

Serapis: Composite deity who originated in Ptolemaic Egypt. Elements of Classical (Hades, Asclepius, Dionysus) and Egyptian (Osiris, Apis) divinities were combined in this god, who can be identified by the kalathos/modius grain measure he wears as a crown. He often replaced Osiris as the husband of Isis in the goddess' mysteries.

Titans: Group of primordial gods. Among them were Rhea and Cronus, parents of many of the Olympians including Zeus, Hera, Hades, Demeter and Poseidon. In Orphic theogony, the Titans cannibalized the infant Dionysus and were incinerated by Zeus for this killing of his son. From their ashes humankind was created.

Triptolemus: Eleusinian prince and champion of Demeter, who spreads her agricultural arts. Often confused with (although distinct from) his brother Demophoön.

Trophonius: Oracular god from Boeotia. Great and terrifying wonders were experienced by those who descended into his cave sanctuary, so frightening it rendered them unable to speak about the encounter.

Zeus (Jupiter): King of the gods, who ruled from Mount Olympus. This thunderous sky deity was father to many a hero via his numerous extramarital affairs (much to the displeasure of his wife Hera). His symbols were the thunderbolt, oak tree, bull and eagle. A Roman mystery cult was based on a martial aspect of the god, Jupiter Dolichenus.

REFERENCES

1 WHAT IS A MYSTERY RELIGION?

1 Jaan Puhvel, *The Hittite Etymological Dictionary* (Berlin, 1984), pp. 188–92.
2 Hugh Bowden, *Mystery Cults of the Ancient World* (Princeton, NJ, 2010), pp. 14–15.
3 Barry Powell, *Classical Myth*, 6th edn (New York, 2010), p. 235.
4 Beryl Rawson, *Children and Childhood in Roman Italy* (Oxford, 2003), pp. 136–7.
5 Bowden, *Mystery Cults*, pp. 15–18.
6 Dio Chrysostom 12.33, trans. in Bowden, *Mystery Cults*, p. 215.
7 Pausanias, *Description of Greece* 2.17.4.
8 Bowden, *Mystery Cults*, p. 38.
9 See Guy MacLean Rogers, *The Mysteries of Artemis of Ephesos: Cult, Polis, and Change in the Graeco-Roman World* (Princeton, NJ, 2013).
10 Nicole Belayche and Francesco Massa, 'Mystery Cults and Visual Language in Graeco-Roman Antiquity: An Introduction', in *Mystery Cults in Visual Representation in Graeco-Roman Antiquity*, ed. Belayche and Massa (Leiden, 2020), p. 13.
11 Bowden, *Mystery Cults*, p. 138.
12 Ibid., p. 23.

2 DEMETER, PERSEPHONE AND THE ELEUSINIAN MYSTERIES

1 Cicero, *De legibus* 2.36, trans. from 'Mysteries at Eleusis: Images of Inscriptions Project', Cornell University Library,

https://digital.library.cornell.edu/collections/eleusis, accessed 23 January 2025.
2 Crinagoras, *Greek Anthology* 11.42, trans. in Hugh Bowden, *Mystery Cults of the Ancient World* (Princeton, NJ, 2010), p. 26.
3 Bowden, *Mystery Cults*, p. 76.
4 Ibid., p. 29.
5 Ibid.
6 Ibid., p. 33.
7 Ibid., p. 26.
8 Homeric Hymn to Demeter, 235–40, trans. in Jules Cashford, *The Homeric Hymns* (London, 2003).
9 Cashford, *The Homeric Hymns*, 270–75.
10 Ibid., 365–70.
11 Ibid., 470–80.
12 Isocrates, *Panegyricus* 28–9, trans. in Emily Kearns, *Ancient Greek Religion: A Sourcebook* (Hoboken, NJ, 2010), p. 317.
13 Bowden, *Mystery Cults*, p. 31.
14 Diodorus Siculus, *Bibliotheca Historica* 4.14.3.
15 Bowden, *Mystery Cults*, p. 32.
16 Plutarch, *Life of Demetrius* 26.
17 Plato, Gorg. 497c., trans. in Bowden, *Mystery Cults*, p. 32.
18 Bowden, *Mystery Cults*, p. 31.
19 Sarah Pomeroy, *Goddesses, Whores, Wives, and Slaves: Women in Classical Antiquity* (Charlottesville, VA, 1975), p. 77.
20 Ibid.
21 Bowden, *Mystery Cults*, p. 31.
22 Ibid.
23 Pausanias, *Description of Greece* 1.2.4.
24 Aristophanes, *The Frogs* 316ff., trans. Eugene O'Neill, 'Iakkhos', *Theoi*, www.theoi.com, accessed 23 January 2025.
25 Pausanias, *Description of Greece* 1.14.1–3, trans. W.H.S. Jones, 'Demeter Cult', *Theoi*, www.theoi.com, accessed 23 January 2025.
26 Bowden, *Mystery Cults*, p. 34.
27 Aristophanes, *Peace* 374–5, Internet Classics Archive, http://classics.mit.edu, accessed 23 January 2025.
28 'Eubouleus', Theoi, www.theoi.com, accessed 23 January 2025.

29 Michael B. Cosmopoulos, *Bronze Age Eleusis and the Origins of the Eleusinian Mysteries* (Cambridge, 2015), p. 13.
30 'Pig, offering to Demeter', https://global.museum-digital.org/object/1486916, accessed 23 January 2025.
31 Cosmopoulos, *Bronze Age Eleusis*, p. 18.
32 Ibid.
33 Ibid., p. 19.
34 Ibid.
35 Ibid.
36 Ibid.
37 Ibid.
38 Ibid., p. 20.
39 Ibid., p. 21.
40 Ibid.
41 Bowden, *Mystery Cults*, p. 37.
42 Sopater, *Rhetores Graeci* 8, trans. in Walter Burkert, *Ancient Mystery Cults* (Cambridge, MA, 1987), p. 90.
43 Bowden, *Mystery Cults*, p. 38.
44 Cosmopoulos, *Bronze Age Eleusis*, p. 22.
45 Plutarch, *Moralia*, frg 178, trans. in F. H. Sandbach, *Moralia*, vol. XV: *Fragments* (Cambridge, MA, 1969).
46 Cosmopoulos, *Bronze Age Eleusis*, p. 23.
47 Ibid.
48 Ibid.
49 George E. Mylonas, *Eleusis and the Eleusinian Mysteries* (Princeton, NJ, 1961), pp. 273–4, 303–5.
50 Bowden, *Mystery Cults*, p. 24.
51 Cosmopoulos, *Bronze Age Eleusis*, p. 24.
52 Ibid.
53 *Zeitschrift für Papyrologie und Epigraphik*, 47, trans. in Simon Price, *Religions of the Ancient Greeks* (Cambridge, 1999), p. 114.
54 Herodotus, *Histories* 6.75.3; 9.65.2.
55 Livy, *History of Rome* XXXI, 14.
56 Bowden, *Mystery Cults*, pp. 38–9.
57 Athenagoras, *A Plea for the Christians* 4, trans. Benjamin Plummer Pratten (1885), Christian Classics Ethereal Library, https://ccel.org/ccel/schaff/anf02/anf02.v.ii.iv.html.
58 Clement of Alexandria, *Protrepticus*, 2, trans. G. W. Butterworth (Cambridge, MA, 1919), p. 31.

59 Ibid.
60 Kevin Clinton, 'The Mysteries of Demeter and Kore', in *A Companion to Greek Religion*, ed. Daniel Ogden (Hoboken , NJ, 2010), pp. 349–53.
61 Sophocles, Fragment 837 Radt, trans. in Helene P. Foley, *The Homeric Hymn to Demeter: Translation, Commentary, and Interpretive Essays* (Princeton, NJ, 1994), p. 70.
62 Notably a Roman example held by the Metropolitan Museum of Art (accession no. 14.130.9).
63 Pausanias, *Description of Greece* 8.15.1–3.
64 Pausanias, *Description of Greece* 4.1.5–9; 4.2.6; 4.26.6–8.
65 Marvin W. Meyer, *The Ancient Mysteries: A Sourcebook of Sacred Texts* (Philadelphia, PA, 1987), pp. 51–9.
66 Trans. in Bowden, *Mystery Cults*, pp. 69–70.
67 Bowden, *Mystery Cults*, p. 70.
68 Pausanias, *Description of Greece* 8.37.8, trans. ibid., p. 74.
69 Artemis has been proposed as a candidate, but this seems unlikely.
70 Jan N. Bremmer, *Initiation into the Mysteries of the Ancient World* (Berlin, 2014), p. 83.
71 Pausanias, *Description of Greece* 8.42.3–5, trans. W.H.S. Jones (1918), www.perseus.tufts.edu/hopper/text?doc= Perseus:text:1999.01.0160.
72 E. W. Averett, 'Theriomorphic Figures in Hellenistic and Roman Arcadia: Nostalgia and Ritual', in *Hellenistic and Roman Terracottas*, ed. Giorgos Papantoniou, Demetrios Michaelides and Maria Dikomitou-Eliadou (Leiden, 2019), pp. 165–71.

3 GRECO-ROMAN EGYPTOMANIA: ISIS AND SERAPIS

1 Hugh Bowden, *Mystery Cults of the Ancient World* (Princeton, NJ, 2010), p. 178.
2 Ibid., p. 157.
3 Plutarch, *Moralia, On Isis and Osiris*.
4 Bowden, *Mystery Cults*, p. 159.
5 Ibid.
6 Ibid., p. 160.
7 Ibid., p. 157.

8 Ibid., p. 161.
9 Trans. in Marvin W. Meyer, *The Ancient Mysteries: A Sourcebook of Sacred Texts* (Philadelphia, PA, 1987), pp. 173–4.
10 Jaime Alvar, *Romanising Oriental Gods* (Leiden, 2008), pp. 314–15.
11 As apparent in both visual evidence and Apuelius' *Metamorphoses* Book XI.
12 Bowden, *Mystery Cults*, p. 165.
13 Sandra Sandri, 'Terracottas', in *The Oxford Handbook of Roman Egypt*, ed. Christina Riggs (Oxford, 2012), p. 637.
14 Pausanias, *Description of Greece* 10.32.12–18.
15 Bowden, *Mystery Cults*, p. 161.
16 Alvar, *Romanising Oriental Gods*, p. 296.
17 Apuleius, *Metamorphoses* 11.16, trans. ibid., p. 298.
18 Richard Veymiers, 'Introduction Agents, Images, Practices', in *Individuals and Materials in the Greco-Roman Cults of Isis*, ed. V. Gasparini and R. Veymiers (Leiden, 2018), p. 1.
19 Josephus, *Antiquity of the Jews* 18.65–79.
20 Jan N. Bremmer, *Initiation into the Mysteries of the Ancient World* (Berlin, 2014), p. 116.
21 Pausanias, *Description of Greece* 10.32.9.
22 As apparent in Apuleius' defence speech, the *Apologia*, when he was put on trial for witchcraft in AD 158–9.
23 Apuleius, *Metamorphoses* 11.22, trans. in Bremmer, *Initiation into the Mysteries*, p. 118.
24 Ibid., 11.23, p. 121.
25 Bremmer, *Initiation into the Mysteries*, p. 123.
26 Meyer, *The Ancient Mysteries*, p. 159.
27 Bremmer, *Initiation into the Mysteries*, p. 121.
28 Bowden, *Mystery Cults*, p. 72.
29 Ibid.

4 MITHRAISM: A BOYS' CLUB

1 Hugh Bowden, *Mystery Cults of the Ancient World* (Princeton, NJ, 2010), p. 181.
2 Andrew Fear, *Mithras* (London, 2022), p. 47.
3 Ibid.
4 Most notably Franz Cumont, *Les religions orientales dans le paganisme romain* (Paris, 1929).

5 Fear, *Mithras*, p. 43.
6 Manfred Clauss, *The Roman Cult of Mithras: The God and His Mysteries* (New York, 2001), p. xxi.
7 Bowden, *Mystery Cults*, p. 182.
8 Jan N. Bremmer, *Initiation into the Mysteries of the Ancient World* (Berlin, 2014), p. 131.
9 Clauss, *The Roman Cult of Mithras*, p. 43.
10 Ibid., p. 53.
11 Trans. in Roger Beck, 'Ritual, Myth, Doctrine, and Initiation in the Mysteries of Mithras: New Evidence from a Cult Vessel', *Journal of Roman Studies*, XC (2000), p. 147.
12 Clauss, *The Roman Cult of Mithras*, pp. 77–8.
13 Ibid., p. 82.
14 Ibid., pp. 95–8.
15 Bowden, *Mystery Cults*, p. 185.
16 Ibid., p. 187.
17 Clauss, *The Roman Cult of Mithras*, pp. 79–80.
18 Ibid., p. 52.
19 Bowden, *Mystery Cults*, p. 187.
20 Clauss, *The Roman Cult of Mithras*, p. 148.
21 Ibid., p. 84.
22 Bowden, *Mystery Cults*, p. 189.
23 Richard Gordon, 'From East to West: Staging Religious Experience in the Mithraic Temple', in *Entangled Worlds: Religious Confluences between East and West in the Roman Empire*, ed. S. Nagel, J. F. Quack and C. Witschel (Tübingen, 2017), p. 425.
24 Bowden, *Mystery Cults*, p. 190.
25 Gordon, 'From East to West', pp. 432–3.
26 Clauss, *The Roman Cult of Mithras*, p. 120.
27 Ibid., p. 61.
28 Ibid., p. 66.
29 Fear, *Mithras*, p. 76.
30 Ibid., p. 79.
31 Another version of the legend held that Tarpeia sold out her city for love.
32 The new legend MITHRAS OROMASDES was punched around its rim. The Greek word PHREN runs across the centre.
33 Clauss, *The Roman Cult of Mithras*, pp. 71–4.
34 Ibid., p. 73.

35 Fear, *Mithras*, pp. 153–4.
36 Ibid., p. 83.
37 Clauss, *The Roman Cult of Mithras*, p. 164.
38 Ibid., p. 164.
39 Ibid., pp. 162–7.
40 Ibid., pp. 151–2.
41 The Sun and Moon were regarded in the Classical world as planets. Uranus, Neptune and Pluto were yet to be discovered.
42 Bowden, *Mystery Cults*, p. 193.
43 Bremmer, *Initiation into the Mysteries*, p. 134.
44 Ibid.
45 Clauss, *The Roman Cult of Mithras*, pp. 33–41.
46 Ibid., p. 143.
47 Ibid., pp. 39–41.
48 Fear, *Mithras*, pp. 34–6.
49 Ibid., pp. 30–41.
50 Ibid., p. 22.
51 Ibid., pp. 19–20.
52 Ibid., p. 22.
53 A. B. Griffith, 'Completing the Picture: Women and the Female Principle in the Mithraic Cult', *Numen*, LIII (2006), pp. 66–7.
54 Ibid., p. 77.
55 Porphyry, *De Antro Nympharum* 15.
56 Tertullian, *De Corona* 15.3, trans. in Bowden, *Mystery Cults*, p. 192.
57 Clauss, *The Roman Cult of Mithras*, pp. 102–3.
58 Ibid., p. 103.
59 Richard Gordon, 'Temporary Deprivation: Rules and Meanings', in *A Companion to the Archaeology of Religion in the Ancient World*, ed. R. Raja and J. Rüpke (Hoboken, NJ, 2015), p. 201.
60 Trans. adapted from Bremmer, *Initiation into the Mysteries*, p. 133.
61 Clauss, *The Roman Cult of Mithras*, p. 133.
62 Bremmer, *Initiation into the Mysteries*, p. 133.
63 Beck, 'Ritual, Myth, Doctrine, and Initiation in the Mysteries of Mithras', pp. 145–80.
64 Ibid., pp. 150–52.

65 Julian, *The Caesars* 336c, trans. in María Pilar García Ruiz, 'The Caesars: A Myth on Julian's Emperorship', in *Emperors and Emperorship in Late Antiquity*, ed. M. P. García Ruiz and A. J. Quiroga Puertas (Leiden, 2020), p. 109.
66 Marvin W. Meyer, *The Ancient Mysteries: A Sourcebook of Sacred Texts* (Philadelphia, PA, 1987), pp. 209–10.
67 Fear, *Mithras*, p. 125.
68 Ibid., p. 177.
69 Based on author's visit to the site in June 2023.
70 Nadežda Gavrilović Vitas, *Ex Asia et Syria: Oriental Religions in the Roman Central Balkans* (Oxford, 2021), pp. 92–113.
71 As is the case for Bronze Age depictions of the Hittite storm-god Teshub.

5 THE SAMOTHRACIAN MYSTERIES AND THE KABEIROI

1 Hugh Bowden, *Mystery Cults of the Ancient World* (Princeton, NJ, 2010), p. 49.
2 Plutarch, *Life of Alexander* 2.1.
3 Herodotus, *Histories* 2.51.
4 Ibid.
5 Thucydides, *History of the Peloponnesian War* 6.27.
6 Pausanias, *Description of Greece* 9.25.6, trans. in Bowden, *Mystery Cults*, p. 57.
7 Marvin W. Meyer, *The Ancient Mysteries: A Sourcebook of Sacred Texts* (Philadelphia, PA, 1987), p. 39.
8 Jan N. Bremmer, *Initiation into the Mysteries of the Ancient World* (Berlin, 2014), pp. 34–5.
9 Bowden, *Mystery Cults*, p. 63.
10 Ibid., p. 65.
11 Susan Guettel Cole, *Theoi Megaloi: The Cult of the Great Gods at Samothrace* (Leiden, 2015), pp. 87–103.
12 Diodorus Siculus, *Bibliotheca Historica* 5.49.5, trans. in Meyer, *The Ancient Mysteries*, pp. 38–41.
13 Bowden, *Mystery Cults*, p. 66.
14 Diogenes Laertius, *Vitae Philosophorum* 6.59, trans. in Bremmer, *Initiation into the Mysteries*, p. 29.
15 Simon Price, *Religions of the Ancient Greeks* (Cambridge, 1999), p. 112.

16 Ibid.
17 Bowden, *Mystery Cults*, p. 52.
18 Tacitus, *Annales* 2.54.2–4.
19 Bremmer, *Initiation into the Mysteries*, p. 27.
20 Price, *Religions of the Ancient Greeks*, p. 112.
21 Kevin Clinton, 'Stages of Initiation in the Eleusinian and Samothracian Mysteries', in *Greek Mysteries: The Archaeology and Ritual of Ancient Secret Cults*, ed. Michael B. Cosmopoulos (London, 2003), pp. 61–2.
22 Ibid.
23 Bremmer, *Initiation into the Mysteries*, p. 26.
24 Clinton, 'Stages of Initiation', p. 67.
25 Ibid.
26 Ibid., pp. 67–9.
27 Bremmer, *Initiation into the Mysteries*, p. 29.
28 Ibid.
29 Ibid., p. 33.

6 ORPHISM AND THE DIONYSIAN MYSTERIES

1 Marvin W. Meyer, *The Ancient Mysteries: A Sourcebook of Sacred Texts* (Philadelphia, PA, 1987), p. 63.
2 Pseudo-Apollodorus, *Bibliotheca* 2.191–2.
3 Plato, *Phaedo* 9c, trans. Harold North Fowler, *Plato in Twelve Volumes*, vol. 1 (Cambridge, MA, 1966).
4 Hugh Bowden, *Mystery Cults of the Ancient World* (Princeton, NJ, 2010), p. 106.
5 Ibid., p. 135.
6 Ibid., p. 136.
7 Ibid., p. 134.
8 Ibid., pp. 105–9.
9 Barry Powell, *Classical Myth*, 6th edn (New York, 2010), p. 278.
10 Pseudo-Apollodorus, *Bibliotheca* 3.26–7.
11 Diodorus Siculus, *Bibliotheca Historica* 3.62.5.
12 Meyer, *The Ancient Mysteries*, p. 163.
13 Bowden, *Mystery Cults*, p. 123.
14 Euripides, *Bacchae* 73–87, trans. Theodore Alois W. Buckley, *The Tragedies of Euripides* (Oxford, 1850).
15 Ibid., 472–4.
16 Pseudo-Apollodorus, *Bibliotheca* 3.38.

17 This metaphor was also associated with Dionysus' dismemberment by the Titans, as noted in Diodorus Siculus, *Bibliotheca Historica* 3.62.
18 Richard Seaford, *Dionysos* (London, 2006), p. 52.
19 Ibid., p. 61.
20 Apuleius, *Apologia* 55, trans. H. E. Butler in *Apuleius, Apology and Florida* (Oxford, 1909).
21 Bowden, *Mystery Cults*, p. 121.
22 Plutarch, *Moralia* 953d, 249e.
23 Pausanias, *Description of Greece* 3.20.3.
24 Bowden, *Mystery Cults*, p. 125.
25 Ibid., p. 126.
26 Livy, *History of Rome* 39.8, trans. adapted from William Heinemann, *The History of Rome, Books XXXVIII–XXXIX, by Titus Livius* (London, 1936).
27 Bowden, *Mystery Cults*, pp. 124–5.
28 Ibid.
29 Bowden, *Mystery Cults*, p. 130.
30 Meyer, *The Ancient Mysteries*, p. 64.
31 Seaford, *Dionysos*, p. 62.
32 Bremmer, *Initiation into the Mysteries*, p. 107.
33 Ibid., p. 105.
34 Bowden, *Mystery Cults*, pp. 130, 113.
35 Seaford, *Dionysos*, pp. 64–5.
36 Ibid., p. 66.
37 Volute Krater (Mixing Vessel) with Dionysus Visiting Hades and Persephone, Toledo Museum of Art, 1994.19.
38 Seaford, *Dionysos*, pp. 79–80.
39 Horace, *Odes* 2.19, trans. adapted from Joseph P. Clancy, *Odes and Epodes* (Chicago, IL, 1960).
40 Seaford, *Dionysos*, p. 69.
41 Ibid.
42 Ibid.
43 Ibid., p. 79.
44 For a full study of these red-figure vessels, see David Saunders, *Underworld: Imagining the Afterlife in Ancient South Italian Vase Painting* (Los Angeles, CA, 2022).
45 'Orphism', *Tate*, www.tate.org.uk, accessed 23 January 2025.
46 Bremmer, *Initiation into the Mysteries*, p. 57.
47 Virgil, *Georgics* 4.517–27.

48 Bowden, *Mystery Cults*, p. 140.
49 Bremmer, *Initiation into the Mysteries*, pp. 62–3.
50 Powell, *Classical Myth*, pp. 300–301.
51 Bremmer, *Initiation into the Mysteries*, pp. 67–70.
52 Aristotle's *On the Pythagoreans* (frg 195) appears to claim that beans function as a gateway for transporting souls to Hades. In Pliny's *Natural History* (XVIII, 118) Varro likewise reports that beans contain the souls of the dead.
53 Trans. in Apostolos N. Athanassakis and Benjamin M. Wolkow, *The Orphic Hymns* (Baltimore, MD, 2013), p. 38.
54 Trans. in Alberto Bernabé and Ana Isabel Jiménez San Cristóbal, *Instructions for the Netherworld* (Leiden, 2007), p. 75.
55 Roy D. Kotansky, 'Dialogues of the Dead on the "Orphic" Gold Tablets', in *Underworld*, ed. Saunders, pp. 29–30.
56 Bowden, *Mystery Cults*, p. 152.
57 As in the example of the tablet from Petelia of the third–second century BC. British Museum (1843,0724.3).
58 Bernabé and San Cristóbal, *Instructions for the Netherworld*, p. 4.
59 Reinhold Merkelbach, 'Die Goldenen Totenpässe: Ägyptisch, Orphisch, Bakchisch', *Zeitschrift für Papyrologie und Epigraphik*, CXXVIII (1999), pp. 1–13.
60 Bernabé and San Cristóbal, *Instructions for the Netherworld*, pp. 29–30.
61 Ibid., pp. 32–4.
62 Homer, *Odyssey* 11.1–50.
63 Bernabé and San Cristóbal, *Instructions for the Netherworld*, p. 227.
64 Kotansky, 'Dialogues of the Dead', pp. 32–3, 35, 38–9.
65 Saunders, ed., *Underworld*, p. 151.
66 Fritz Graf, 'Text and ritual: The Corpus Eschatologicum of the Orphics', in *The 'Orphic' Gold Tablets and Greek Religion*, ed. Radcliffe G. Edmonds (Cambridge, 2011), p. 56.
67 Bowden, *Mystery Cults*, p. 151.
68 Bernabé and San Cristóbal, *Instructions for the Netherworld*, p. 161.
69 Bowden, *Mystery Cults*, p. 155.
70 M. A. Santamaría Álvarez, ed., *The Derveni Papyrus: Unearthing Ancient Mysteries* (Leiden, 2018), p. 1.

71 Bremmer, *Initiation into the Mysteries*, p. 63.
72 Carlos Megino Rodríguez, 'Daimons in the Derveni Papyrus and in Early Stoicism', in *The Derveni Papyrus*, ed. Santamaría Álvarez, p. 34.
73 Bremmer, *Initiation into the Mysteries*, p. 70.
74 Bowden, *Mystery Cults*, p. 144.
75 Bremmer, *Initiation into the Mysteries*, pp. 67–8.
76 Iamblichus, *On the Pythagorean Life* 82–6.
77 Aristotle, *Metaphysics* 1.5, trans. W. D. Ross, *Metaphysics* (Oxford, 1924).
78 Bowden, *Mystery Cults*, p. 146.
79 Ibid.
80 Herodotus, *Histories* 2.81.
81 Aristotle, Fr. 191.
82 Ibid.
83 Pausanias, *Description of Greece* 9.37.4.
84 Ibid., 9.39.3.
85 Yulia Ustinova, *Caves and the Ancient Greek Mind* (Oxford, 2009), pp. 91–2.
86 Pausanias, *Description of Greece* 9.39.3.
87 Ibid.
88 Aristophanes, *Clouds* 506, trans. William James Hickie in *The Comedies of Aristophanes* (London, 1853).
89 Pausanias, *Description of Greece* 9.39.3.
90 Plutarch, *Moralia, De Genio Socratis* 22, trans. William W. Godwin, *Plutarch's Morals* (Oxford, 1874).

7 GODS FROM ANATOLIA

1 Gaea (goddess of the Earth), Rhea (Titan goddess, who was mother to the gods Zeus, Hera, Demeter, Hades, Poseidon and Hestia), Hera (Queen of the Gods) and Demeter (fertility goddess of the life-giving harvest) have all been described in Classical sources as such. See Hugh Bowden, *Mystery Cults of the Ancient World* (Princeton, NJ, 2010), pp. 84–5.
2 Appian, *Roman History* 7.9.56; Herodian, *History of the Empire* 1.11.1.
3 Ovid, *Fasti* 4.291–348.
4 Marvin W. Meyer, *The Ancient Mysteries: A Sourcebook of Sacred Texts* (Philadelphia, PA, 1987), p. 113.

5 Bowden, *Mystery Cults*, p. 85.
6 Damien Stone, *The Hittites* (London, 2023), p. 160.
7 Plato, *Euthyphro* 277d, trans. in Bowden, *Mystery Cults*, p. 91.
8 Dionysius of Halicarnassus, *Roman Antiquities* 2.19.3–5.
9 The best account is provided by the recent Christian convert Arnobius of Sicca (third century AD) in *The Case against the Pagans*, Book v.5–7. See Meyer, *The Ancient Mysteries*, pp. 116–19.
10 Pausanias, *Description of Greece* 7.17.8.
11 Strabo, *Geography* 10.3.12; 12.5.3.
12 Pausanias, *Description of Greece* 7.19.9–12.
13 Arnobius of Sicca, *Case against the Pagans* 5.7.
14 Bowden, *Mystery Cults*, p. 88.
15 Lynn E. Roller, *In Search of God the Mother: The Cult of Anatolian Cybele* (Oakland, CA, 1999), pp. 162–7.
16 Bowden, *Mystery Cults*, p. 88.
17 Meyer, *The Ancient Mysteries*, p. 114.
18 Ibid.
19 Ibid.
20 It's probable that many galli followed Attis to the Underworld as a result of this frenzied mutilation.
21 Meyer, *The Ancient Mysteries*, p. 114.
22 Françoise Van Haeperen, 'The Cista, a Hallmark of Mater Magna's Mysteries in the Roman World?', in *Mystery Cults in Visual Representation in Graeco-Roman Antiquity*, ed. N. Belayche and F. Massa (Leiden, 2020), p. 213.
23 Ibid., p. 199.
24 Valerius Maximus, *De Factis Dictisque Memorabilibus* 7.7.6, trans. S. Speed, *Factorum et dictorum memorabilium libri IX* (London, 1678).
25 Catullus, *Poem 64*, trans. in Meyer, *The Ancient Mysteries*, p. 126.
26 Firmicus Maternus, *De errore profanarum religionum* 4.1–2, trans. C. Forbes, *The Error of the Pagan Religions* (New York, 1970).
27 Shelley J. Hales, 'Looking for Eunuchs: The Galli and Attis in Roman Art', in *Eunuchs in Antiquity and Beyond*, ed. S. Tougher (London, 2002), p. 91.

28 Maarten J. Vermaseren, *Cybele and Attis: The Myth and The Cult* (London, 1977), p. 96.
29 Meyer, *The Ancient Mysteries*, p. 147.
30 Prudentius, *Crowns of Martyrdom*, x.1005–50, trans. H. J. Thomson, *Prudentius*, vol. II (Cambridge, MA, 1953).
31 Jeremy Rutter, 'The Three Phases of the Taurobolium', *Phoenix*, XXII/3 (1968), pp. 237–8.
32 Ibid., p. 233.
33 Susanne Berndt Ersöz, 'The Hand Gesture and Symbols of Sabazios', *Opuscula: Annual of the Swedish Institutes at Athens and Rome*, XI (2018), p. 153.
34 Walters Art Museum Accession no. 54.2453.
35 Ersöz, 'The Hand Gesture', p. 162.
36 Ibid., p. 151.
37 Ibid., p. 154.

8 GLYCON; OR, HOW TO START YOUR OWN RELIGIOUS CULT IN ANTIQUITY

1 Plato, *Republic* 364b, trans. in Hugh Bowden, *Mystery Cults of the Ancient World* (Princeton, NJ, 2010), p. 139.
2 Lucian, *Alexander* 16, trans. in Wiebke Friese, 'Trick or Treat? Secrecy and Performative Space in the Sanctuary of Glycon Neos Asclepius', in *Revealing and Concealing in Antiquity: Textual and Archaeological Approaches to Secrecy*, ed. E. Mortensen and S. G. Saxkjær (Aarhus, 2015), p. 155.
3 Christopher P. Jones, *Culture and Society in Lucian* (Cambridge, MA, 1986), p. 143.
4 Lucian, *Alexander* 39.
5 Lucian, *Alexander* 16, trans. in Friese, 'Trick or Treat?', pp. 151–2.
6 His most famous patient was Aelius Aristides, a hypochondriac who frequented the Asclepieion. Between AD 130 and 171 he received 130 dreams from the god of healing, which Aristides recorded in a work that is now known as the *Sacred Tales*.
7 John Murray, *A Dictionary of Greek and Roman Antiquities* (London, 1875), p. 288.
8 Gaston H. Halsberghe, *The Cult of Sol Invictus* (Leiden, 1972), p. 61.

9 Herodian, *History of the Empire* 5.3.2, trans. in Martijn Icks, *The Crimes of Elagabalus: The Life and Legacy of Rome's Decadent Boy Emperor* (Cambridge, MA, 2012), p. 89.
10 Pierre M. Bellemare, 'Meteorite Sparks a Cult', *Journal of the Royal Astronomical Society of Canada*, XC/5–6 (1996), pp. 287–91.
11 Halsberghe, *The Cult of Sol Invictus*, pp. 91–5.
12 Herodian, *History of the Empire* 5.6.
13 Halsberghe, *The Cult of Sol Invictus*, pp. 82–3, 95.
14 Historia Augusta, *Life of Elagabalus* 3.4, trans. David Magie, *Historia Augusta*, vol. I (Cambridge, MA, 1924).
15 Halsberghe, *The Cult of Sol Invictus*, pp. 76, 104.
16 Historia Augusta, *Life of Elagabalus* 8.1; Cassius Dio, *Roman History* 80.11.1.
17 Historia Augusta, *Life of Elagabalus* 27.4.
18 The conceptual artist Sophie Calle adopted a comparable eating regime in her 1998 artwork *The Chromatic Diet*. Recording her meals in a photo journal, each day Calle only ate foods of a single colour.

9 FROM EARLY CHRISTIANITY TO MODERNITY

1 Both papers are available via Stanford's Martin Luther King Jr Research and Education Centre. Accessible online at https://kinginstitute.stanford.edu.
2 'I am the light of the world' (John 8:12; 9:5; 12:46).
3 Hugh Bowden, *Mystery Cults of the Ancient World* (Princeton, NJ, 2010), pp. 208–9.
4 Pseudo-Dionysius, *The Ecclesiastical Hierarchy* 372a4, trans. Colm Luibheid, *Pseudo-Dionysius: The Complete Works* (Mahwah, NJ, 1987).
5 Minucius Felix, *Octavius* 9.7, trans. Robert Ernest Wallis, *The Ante-Nicene Fathers*, vol. IV (Buffalo, NY, 1885).
6 Bowden, *Mystery Cults*, p. 208.
7 James Stephen Curl, *The Egyptian Revival: Ancient Egypt as the Inspiration for Design Motifs in the West* (New York, 2005), pp. 62–4.
8 Justin Martyr, *Apologies* 1.54.
9 Philo of Alexandria, *De Vita Contemplativa*, trans. F. H. Colson (1941) in Marvin W. Meyer, *The Ancient Mysteries: A Sourcebook of Sacred Texts* (Philadelphia, PA, 1987), p. 230.

10 Andrew Fear, *Mithras* (London, 2022), p. 6.
11 Bowden, *Mystery Cults*, pp. 217–21.
12 Fear, *Mithras*, p. 199.
13 Bowden, *Mystery Cults*, p. 214.
14 Dipinti from the Mithraeum of Santa Prisca.
15 One can put in an application for Bacchanalia's dining club 'Apollo's Muse' at https://apply.apollos-muse.co.uk/memberships.
16 Aleister Crowley, *The Rites of Eleusis* (London, 1910).
17 Text from blurb of Kim Antieau, *The Salmon Mysteries: A Guidebook to a Reimagining of the Eleusinian Mysteries* (ebook, 2010).
18 Yulia Ustinova, *Caves and the Ancient Greek Mind* (Oxford, 2009), p. 231.

SELECT BIBLIOGRAPHY

Alvar, Jaime, *Romanising Oriental Gods* (Leiden, 2008)

Athanassakis, A. N., and B. M. Wolkow, *The Orphic Hymns* (Baltimore, MD, 2013)

Beck, Roger, 'Ritual, Myth, Doctrine, and Initiation in the Mysteries of Mithras: New Evidence from a Cult Vessel', *Journal of Roman Studies*, XC (2000), pp. 145–80

Belayche, Nicole, and Francesco Massa, 'Mystery Cults and Visual Language in Graeco-Roman Antiquity: An Introduction', in *Mystery Cults in Visual Representation in Graeco-Roman Antiquity*, ed. N. Belayche and F. Massa (Leiden, 2020), pp. 1–37

Bellemare, Pierre M., 'Meteorite Sparks a Cult', *Journal of the Royal Astronomical Society of Canada*, XC/5–6 (1996), pp. 287–91

Bernabé, Alberto, and Ana Isabel Jiménez San Cristóbal, *Instructions for the Netherworld* (Leiden, 2007)

Berndt Ersöz, Susanne, 'The Hand Gesture and Symbols of Sabazios', *Opuscula: Annual of the Swedish Institutes at Athens and Rome*, XI (2018), pp. 151–68

Bowden, Hugh, *Mystery Cults of the Ancient World* (Princeton, NJ, 2010)

Bremmer, Jan, *Initiation into the Mysteries of the Ancient World* (Berlin, 2015)

Burkert, Walter, *Ancient Mystery Cults* (Cambridge, MA, 1989)

Clauss, Manfred, *The Roman Cult of Mithras: The God and His Mysteries* (New York, 2001)

Clinton, Kevin, 'The Mysteries of Demeter and Kore', in *A Companion to Greek Religion*, ed. D. Ogden, 1st edn (Oxford, 2007), pp. 342–56

—, 'Stages of Initiation in the Eleusinian and Samothracian Mysteries', in *Greek Mysteries: The Archaeology of Ancient Greek Secret Cults*, ed. M. B. Cosmopoulos (London, 2002), pp. 50–78

Cosmopoulos, Michael B., *Bronze Age Eleusis and the Origins of the Eleusinian Mysteries* (Cambridge, 2015)

Fear, Andrew, *Mithras* (London, 2022)

Friese, Wiebke, 'Trick or Treat? Secrecy and Performative Space in the Sanctuary of Glycon Neos Asclepius', in *Revealing and Concealing in Antiquity: Textual and Archaeological Approaches to Secrecy*, ed. E. Mortensen and S. G. Saxkjær (Aarhus, 2015), pp. 147–60

Gordon, R., 'From East to West: Staging Religious Experience in the Mithraic Temple', in *Entangled Worlds: Religious Confluences between East and West in the Roman Empire*, ed. S. Nagel, J. F. Quack and C. Witschel (Tübingen, 2017), pp. 413–42

—, 'Temporary Deprivation: Rules and Meanings', in *A Companion to the Archaeology of Religion in the Ancient World*, ed. R. Raja and J. Rüpke (Hoboken, NJ, 2015), pp. 194–206

Graf, Fritz, 'Text and Ritual: The Corpus Eschatologicum of the Orphics', in *The 'Orphic' Gold Tablets and Greek Religion*, ed. Radcliffe G. Edmonds (Cambridge, 2011), pp. 53–67

Griffith, A. B., 'Completing the Picture: Women and the Female Principle in the Mithraic Cult', *Numen*, LIII (2006), pp. 48–77

Guettel Cole, Susan, *Theoi Megaloi: The Cult of the Great Gods at Samothrace* (Leiden, 2015)

Hales, Shelley J., 'Looking for Eunuchs: The Galli and Attis in Roman Art', in *Eunuchs in Antiquity and Beyond*, ed. S. Tougher (London, 2002), pp. 87–102

Halsberghe, G., *The Cult of Sol Invictus* (Leiden, 1972)

Icks, Martijn, *The Crimes of Elagabalus: The Life and Legacy of Rome's Decadent Boy Emperor* (Cambridge, MA, 2012)

Jones, Christopher P., *Culture and Society in Lucian* (Cambridge, MA, 1986)

Meyer, Marvin W., *The Ancient Mysteries: A Sourcebook of Sacred Texts* (Philadelphia, PA, 1999)

Mylonas, George E., *Eleusis and the Eleusinian Mysteries* (Princeton, NJ, 1961)

Pomeroy, Sarah, *Goddesses, Whores, Wives, and Slaves: Women in Classical Antiquity* (Charlottesville, VA, 1995)

Powell, Barry, *Classical Myth*, 6th edn (New York, 2010)
Price, Simon, *Religions of the Ancient Greeks* (Cambridge, 1999)
Riggs, Christina, ed., *The Oxford Handbook of Roman Egypt* (Oxford, 2012)
Roller, Lynn E., *In Search of God the Mother: The Cult of Anatolian Cybele* (Oakland, CA, 1999)
Rutter, Jeremy, 'The Three Phases of the Taurobolium', *Phoenix*, XXII/3 (1968), pp. 226–49
Santamaría Álvarez, M. A., ed., *The Derveni Papyrus: Unearthing Ancient Mysteries* (Leiden, 2018)
Saunders, David, ed., *Underworld: Imagining the Afterlife in Ancient South Italian Vase Painting* (Los Angeles, CA, 2022)
Seaford, Richard, *Dionysos* (London, 2006)
Ustinova, Yulia, *Caves and the Ancient Greek Mind* (Oxford, 2009)
Van Haeperen, Françoise, 'The Cista, a Hallmark of Mater Magna's Mysteries in the Roman World?', in *Mystery Cults in Visual Representation in Graeco-Roman Antiquity*, ed. N. Belayche and F. Massa (Leiden, 2020), pp. 194–217
Vermaseren, M. J., *Cybele and Attis: The Myth and the Cult* (London, 1977)
Veymiers, Richard, 'Introduction Agents, Images, Practices', in *Individuals and Materials in the Greco-Roman Cults of Isis*, ed. V. Gasparini and R. Veymiers (Leiden, 2018), pp. 1–58

ACKNOWLEDGEMENTS

First, I would like to thank Michael Leaman and the team at Reaktion Books for enthusiastically taking on this project. Even though we frustrate each other at times, you have been incredibly supportive of all my writing ventures! Gratitude is due to *all* my friends and family for their support. Wendy Stone, Sunnie Ha Nguyen, Liam McGeagh and Martin Prieto Cardone deserve special mention for constantly checking on my progress and just being really great mates. My partner Geoffrey Page was my first initiate, who read the earliest draft of this work and provided invaluable feedback. You have always been patient with my very particular needs and you give me the strength to keep going. Finally, a big thank you to all my colleagues at the Chau Chak Wing Museum for your interest, ideas and expertise. Many of our objects are wonderfully illustrated in these pages. I hope that through this book they (and mystery cults more generally) reach a new audience.

PHOTO ACKNOWLEDGEMENTS

The author and publishers wish to express their thanks to the sources listed below for illustrative material and/or permission to reproduce it. Some locations of artworks are also given below, in the interest of brevity.

Alamy: p. 145 (Jimlop collection); Chau Chak Wing Museum, University of Sydney: pp. 6, 31, 44, 57, 107, 111; Flickr: p. 91 (HEN-Magonza); J. Paul Getty Museum: pp. 51, 121, 126; LACMA (Los Angeles County Museum of Art): p. 58 (Gift of Jerome F. Snyder/ M.80.202.222); Metropolitan Museum of Art: pp. 12 (Rogers Fund, 1922), 16 (Gift of Miss Matilda W. Bruce, 1907), 21 (Fletcher Fund, 1928), 38 (Rogers Fund, 1914), 56 (Gift of C. and E. Canessa, 1919), 138 (Rogers Fund, 1922), 139 (Gift of Henry G. Marquand, 1897), 162 (Purchase, Joseph Pulitzer Bequest Fund, 1955); Walters Art Museum: p. 151 (Museum purchase, 1961/Public Domain); Wikimedia Commons: pp. 9 (Public Domain), 23 (Marie-Lan Nguyen/Public Domain), 37 (George E Koronaios/CC BY-SA 4.0), 42 (Fabien Bièvre-Perrin/CC BY-SA 4.0), 48 (Amphipolis/CC BY-SA 2.0), 50 (Daderot/Public Domain), 52 (Jebulon/Public Domain), 54 (Flickr/ Following Hadrian/CC BY-SA 2.0), 55 (Public Domain), 61 (Gary Todd from Xinzheng, China), 63 (Public Domain), 65 (WolfgangRieger/ Public Domain), 67 (Marie-Lan Nguyen/CC BY 2.5), 70 (Flickr/ Following Hadrian/CC BY-SA 2.0), 71 (Pierre-Selim Huard/Public Domain), 73 (Carole Raddato from Frankfurt, Germany/CC BY-SA 2.0), 74 left and right: (Marie-Lan Nguyen/CC BY 2.5), 76 (Jean-Pol Grandmont/CC BY 3.0), 78 (Yale University Art Gallery/Public Domain), 81 (Marie-Lan Nguyen/Public Domain), 82 (Carole Raddato from Frankfurt, Germany/CC BY-SA 2.0), 83 (Coyau/CC BY-SA

3.0), 85 (Mumbler Jamie/CC BY-SA 2.0), 86 top and bottom (Marie-Lan Nguyen/CC BY 2.5), 87 top and bottom (Marie-Lan Nguyen/CC BY 2.5), 94 (It's No Game/CC BY 2.0), 95 (Wolfgang Sauber/CC BY-SA 4.0), 98 (Zde/CC BY-SA 3.0), 101 (Shonagon/Public Domain), 106 (ArchaiOptix/CC BY-SA 4.0), 108 (ArchaiOptix/CC BY-SA 4.0), 114 (ArchaiOptix/CC BY-SA 4.0), 118 (WolfgangRieger/Public Domain), 119 (WolfgangRieger/Public Domain), 120 (WolfgangRieger/Public Domain), 124 (ArchaiOptix/CC BY-SA 4.0), 127 (The National Museum in Warsaw/Public Domain), 132 (Public Domain), 140 (Giovanni Dall'Orto/Public Domain), 142 (CC BY-SA 4.0), 144 (Saiko/CC BY 3.0), 149 (Jebulon/Public Domain), 150 (Public Domain), 152 (Ángel M. Felicísimo from Mérida, España (CC BY 2.0), 166 (British Museum/Public Domain).

INDEX

Page numbers in *italics* refer to illustrations